OLDER PEOPLE
GIVING CARE

OLDER PEOPLE GIVING CARE

Helping Family and Community

Sally K. Gallagher

AUBURN HOUSE
Westport, Connecticut • London

Library of Congress Cataloging-in-Publication Data

Gallagher, Sally K.
   Older people giving care : helping family and community / Sally K.
Gallagher.
    p. cm.
   Includes bibliographical references (p.   ) and index.
   ISBN 0-86569-233-5 (alk. paper)
   1. Aged volunteers in social service – United States.
  2. Caregivers – United States. I. Title.
   HV1465.G36 1994
   361.3'7'0846 – dc20   93-9017

British Library Cataloguing in Publication Data is available.

Library of Congress Catalog Card Number: 93-9017
ISBN: 0-86569-233-5

First published in 1994

Auburn House, 88 Post Road West, Westport, CT 06881
An imprint of Greenwood Publishing Group, Inc.

Printed in the United States of America

∞™

The paper used in this book complies with the
Permanent Paper Standard issued by the National
Information Standards Organization (Z39.48-1984).

10 9 8 7 6 5 4 3 2 1

For my mother,
Charlotte M. Zook,
who has not grown weary of doing good
and who knows who her neighbor is.
(2 Thessalonians 3: 13, Luke 10)

Contents

PART IV: CONCLUSIONS   139

Tables

Preface

Like much social research, this study grew out of private experience as well as public concerns. For as long as I can remember, I have listened as my mother's circle of friends discussed their work as volunteers. I listened with mild interest as they talked about the work itself and, as a sociologist, with greater interest, as they discussed the growing difficulty they faced in recruiting volunteers. Increasingly, they found that younger women with school-age children were employed and either unable or unwilling to add another job to the ones they were already doing. As a result, equitably distributing the work among older volunteers—and retaining them—was becoming more and more important if the calls, the meals, the decorations, the planning, the invitations, the transportation, the visiting were to be done. And I listened, as they did, to news of funding cutbacks and renewed emphasis on public policy encouraging greater reliance on families and volunteers to care for the needy. And I began to wonder, as they (and some of their husbands) did: Who will do this labor? Who will provide this care?

Given the opportunity to work on a larger study on the effects of women's employment on charity work being conducted by Naomi Gerstel at the University of Massachusetts, I decided to examine the largely unseen work that older men and women do in maintaining and supporting the families and communities in which they live. Between the fall of 1987 and January 1989, 324 men and women were interviewed in Springfield, Massachusetts. I conducted nearly all of the interviews myself, and I am deeply grateful to the men and women who opened their homes and their lives to me. This book is, of course, based on those interviews. In writing it, I have often remembered their words and benefitted from their insights.

The text is divided into three sections. Part I provides an introduction to the research as a whole. Chapter 1 outlines some of the theoretical debates and empirical research regarding older men's and women's participation in family and community caregiving. In Chapter 2, I discuss methodology—focusing on sampling, data collection, and areas of measurement used in this analysis. Chapter 3 provides the general context for the rest of the work—focusing in particular on a comparison of the amount of time and types of care older and younger men and women give informally to people they know and to others through formal volunteer activities.

Part II examines the ways in which gender shapes the care older women and men provide. In Chapter 4, I focus on informal help given to family, friends and neighbors, and examine the number of people, amount of time, and range of tasks older women and men perform. Chapter 5 examines the ways in which the characteristics of the recipients shape the care men and women provide to family and friends. In Chapter 6, I turn to help for those who are neither family nor friends, and examine the gender differences in help given others through participation in formal volunteer activities.

Part III extends the analysis to the effects of marriage on older women's giving care. Here, the primary question is the ways in which marriage shapes the help older women give both while they are married and after the loss of a spouse. As in Part II, I first examine informal help to family and friends (Chapter 7) and the ways in which the characteristics of the recipients affect that giving care (Chapter 8). Then, in Chapter 9, I turn to the relationship between marriage and women's helping others through formal volunteer work. Part IV, conclusions, discusses some of the implications of these patterns of help for theories of aging, gender, and marriage as well as public policy emphasizing the role of the elderly in providing unpaid care to both kith and kin.

In studying patterns of support, it is impossible not to be aware of the people who contributed their advice, encouragement and help along the way. I am deeply indebted to Naomi Gerstel, whose scholarship, enthusiasm and careful critique have helped clarify my thinking and writing about these issues. Rick Tessler, Al Cheven, Nylda Glickman, and Andy Anderson also provided important criticism, particularly in the earlier stages of the study. Special thanks are also due Dee Weber for computer programming and technical support; Debbie Sellers for her empathy and encouragement; Anne Balazs for her constructive comments on an earlier version of this manuscript; and Sue Walther and Tom Walther for being good neighbors. I also wish to thank Sigma Xi, the Scientific Research Society, for their grant which helped fund data collection in Springfield.

Finally, I would like to express my appreciation to Laura Porter, whose friendship means a great deal to me; to my mother, for her example in caring for me and others; to my husband, Ed, for his encouragement and patience; and to my son Andrew, who reminds me of other important things, and whose delight at learning rekindles my own.

Part I

Introduction

1

Caring and Giving Care

INTRODUCTION

What does it mean to care for someone? Both popular culture and social research lend themselves to understanding care as having to do with emotions—feelings of affection and concern. Sociologists tell us that this focus on the emotional components of caring is a consequence of industrialization— that in the transition from home to factory production, work and love were also divided. In the process, the home became a "haven" where women specialized in the emotional care and nurturing of its members, while men, at work, focused on instrumental relations and production. In this context, caring has been conceptualized as largely women's domain—"labors of love" not only based on ties of affection, but consisting largely of expressions of intimacy, nurture, and emotion.

Understanding caring as expressions of affection extends to friends as well as family. Caring for friends, particularly among women, began to be idealized during the nineteenth century as an emotional, expressive relation (Cott, 1977). The persistence of this ideal affects popular understanding as well as most recent research on friendship among adults. Women's friendships tend to be characterized in terms of intimacy and affection—the "greeting card" image of women sharing their thoughts and feelings over a cup of coffee. In contrast, men's friendships are described as few and far between—men's relations with other men going unnoticed specifically because they are *not* characterized by affective expressions of intimacy and caring—the signs of "real" friendship (Fox, Gibbs and Auerbach, 1985; Rubin, 1985; Wright, 1989).

These affective expressions of caring for family and friends are considered so fundamental to human society that sociologists have described them as "the nursery of human nature," and the essence of primary group relations (Cooley, 1909; Weber, 1947).[1] Yet this perspective is too narrow. By focusing on the emotional components of caring, the substantial practical labor and material help members of families and communities provide to one another are obscured.

In contrast, enduring norms regarding children's obligation to care for aging parents (Rossi and Rossi, 1990) suggest that caring involves much more than affection. Growing concern over the changing age distribution of the population and the plight of "women in the middle"—caring for two generations of dependents, both children and aging parents (Brody, 1990)—has prompted extensive research examining the tasks involved in caring for the dependent elderly. By concentrating on instrumental tasks, this body of research has shifted the focus from caring as an emotional activity to caring as involving concrete forms of help and support.

This latter body of research also reflects the broader social context in which it has taken place. Changes in the age structure of the population have increased the demand for practical and material care. As the Baby Boom generation ages, the ratio of older dependent parents to wage-earning adult children is expected to shift—causing greater potential burden on a shrinking number of young families. If current birth rates remain the same, the ratio of retirement-age elderly to working-age children will increase from 19 per 100 in 1990 to 37 per 100 in 2030 (U.S. Bureau of the Census, 1988).

At the same time, as more women become employed outside the home, the boundaries between work and family, nurture and instrumentality, blur. Between 1960 and 1991, employment among married women rose from 31.7 to 58.5 percent. Among married women with school-age children, employment increased during these same years from 39 to 72.5 percent (U.S. Bureau of the Census, 1992). Given these broader social and demographic changes, it is not surprising that greater attention is given to the instrumental components of caring.

Because of these demographic changes, it is not surprising that providing care for the dependent elderly should be a major focus of both research and public policy debate. The potential strain an expanding population of elderly puts on the caring resources of others, however, is only part of the picture. Focusing on the elderly solely as recipients of care ignores the potential of the elderly themselves in giving care. Recent polices promoting volunteerism—particularly among the elderly—recognize this potential and suggest that older Americans may be asked to fill in the caregiving gap: to provide the material, practical, and emotional help and support necessary to maintain families and communities. An underlying assumption of these policies is that a significant number of older people are able and willing to give care. Yet, no previous research has examined the degree to which older men and women are involved, or desire to be involved, in giving help and support to family, friends, and others.

This study begins to address these issues by providing an analysis of the amount, range and types of care older men and women provide to kith and kin. The purpose, however, is not only to chronicle the distribution and desire to help, but to analyze the ways in which age, gender, and marriage affect the help given by the elderly. While the analysis focuses primarily on older men and women, the broader question is the degree to which patterns of giving care among the elderly support competing hypotheses about the role of psychosocial development and differing opportunities and constraints in shaping gender roles in adult life. The analysis, therefore, is organized around two axes which are central to the organization of social life—those of gender and marriage. In organizing the analysis in this way, I examine not only the effects of gender and marriage on the help older people give, but also the ways in which patterns of help inform us about sociological theories of gender, marriage, and caring.

Trends in Public Policy

Two related trends in public policy may affect the involvement of the elderly in caring for those in need. The first of these is a declining federal commitment to social welfare spending. During the eighties, the Reagan and Bush administrations reemphasized the role of the private sector by cutting back on funding for social programs and encouraging greater reliance on private charity for meeting social needs. During the 1980s, federal spending for social welfare decreased from 54.3 to 47.7 percent of total government spending and funding for programs for elderly volunteers was reduced 78 percent (U.S. Social Security Administration, 1987).

At the same time as public spending on social welfare was declining, other policies over the past decade promoted greater reliance on the help given by families and through voluntary associations (U.S. Congress, 1989).[2] Following the lead of the Reagan administration, the Bush administration also expressed its commitment to the role of the private sector in meeting social welfare needs. Both George Bush and Barbara Bush expressed their commitment to revitalize volunteerism in America in their campaign rhetoric, television spots, and public addresses. Clearly, the "1000 points of light" campaign reflected the Bush administration's belief that volunteer, private efforts should play a central role in meeting family and community needs. A section from President Bush's 1989 inaugural address makes this particularly clear:

I am speaking of a new engagement in the lives of others—a new activism, hands-on and involved, that gets the job done. We must bring in the generations, harnessing the unused talent of the elderly and the unfocused energy of the young. I have spoken of a thousand points of light—of all the community organizations that are spread like stars throughout the nation doing good. I will go to the people and the programs that are the brighter points of light, and I'll ask every member of my government to become involved. The old ideas are new again because they're not old, they are timeless: duty, sacrifice, commitment and patriotism that finds its expression in taking part and pitching in.

The reference to "harnessing the unused talent of the elderly" reveals the assumption that the resources of the elderly are unused, and that a significant proportion of the elderly possess the skills and desire to perform volunteer work. It is not known, however, how plausible either of these assumptions is.

This commitment to increasing the role of the elderly in volunteerism existed not only in the executive branch, but in the legislature as well. The 1980s and early 1990s saw heated debate over the passing of the Family and Medical Leave Bill mandating that employers provide unpaid leave for childcare and elderly parent care; and the introduction of the New Volunteer Citizens Corps Act—in which young people volunteer in military or civilian programs in return for educational or housing vouchers and older volunteers "work either full- or part-time and would earn a modest hourly wage instead of vouchers. To help keep the program's overhead costs down, many retirees would be assigned to supervisory and administrative positions within the Citizens Corps itself" (U.S. Congress, 1989).

Support for privatized care for the needy also exists on the state level. Most states (70 percent) allow some payment for family services for those who care for disabled elderly at home (Linsk, Keigher, & Osterbusch, 1988). However, payment regulations vary widely and there appears to be little coherent state-level policy regarding family care. Still there does seem to be increasing movement toward supporting families who provide care for those at high risk of institutionalization.

These trends, in particular the previous two administrations' rhetoric and the passing of these bills in the Senate, are indicative of an increasing emphasis on the privatization of care, and the revitalization of volunteerism.

The emphasis on older volunteers is not new, however. Engaging the elderly in local volunteer programs has been on the national agenda since the late 1960s. The first federal program exclusively for elderly volunteers was begun in 1969 (OAVP/ACTION, 1971) and rapidly expanded into three branches: the Retired Senior Volunteer Program, Foster Grandparents, and Senior Companionship Programs. Statistics on volunteer participation were published in the program's newspaper *Prime Time* until 1985, when publication ceased because of cutbacks in federal funding (*Prime Time*, 1985). However at one time more than 320,000 elderly volunteers were active in these programs (OAVP/ACTION, 1982). In 1986 there were over 700 RSVP programs in existence, although not all of these received federal funding (OAVP/ACTION, 1986).

In spite of the dramatic reductions in federal funding for these Older American's Volunteer Programs, the elderly continue to be a target for recruitment in a variety of community-based programs (see Cross et al., 1987; Morrow-Howell and Ozawa, 1987; Scharlach, 1988; Silverman, 1986). While federal policies toward volunteerism among the elderly may seem contradictory—on the one hand, cutting back funding for existing programs; on the other hand, proposing support for new programs—the fact that organizations within the community are promoting older volunteers suggests two things. First, the elderly may indeed have the resources to contribute to community volunteer associations—at least, it may be assumed, the originators of these programs believe them to possess these resources. Second, the establishment of local programs to involve the elderly suggests that older volunteers may be increasingly relied upon to perform social services. This greater reliance on the services of the elderly may be a consequence not only of the privatization of care, but also of greater labor force participation among middle aged women.

Trends in Employment

While women have always been represented in the paid labor force, the past 30 years have seen a marked increase in their participation. Since 1960 the employment of married women with school-age children has almost doubled (U.S. Bureau of Labor Statistics, 1989). A growing volume of research suggests that employment may reduce the supply of those who have traditionally provided the majority of family and community care. Recent research argues that employed women spend less time and provide less hands-on support to family than do homemakers (Gerstel and Gallagher, 1990a). Others argue that employed women are less involved in networks of informal help and exchange with their neighbors (Fischer, 1982; O'Donnell 1985), and spend less time doing volunteer work and directing volunteer associations than do homemakers (Booth, 1972; O'Donnell, 1985).

Since employment reduces the involvement of those traditionally most involved in giving care, needy family and community members may turn to the elderly—those presumably no longer as constrained by the demands of child rearing and employment—to provide the help and support they need.

Trends in Aging

At the same time that public policy and women's employment may be increasing the demand for help given by the elderly, greater longevity and improved health among the elderly may provide a greater potential supply of caregivers. Over the past 30 years, life expectancy has increased from 78 to 80 years of age among men, and from 81 to 84 years of age among women for those 65 or older (U.S. Bureau of the Census, 1992). Older people are not only living longer, they are also in better health at older ages (Fries, 1980).

Overall, these trends in longevity and health, along with the raising of the eligibility age for Social Security and Medicare (*Congressional Quarterly*, 1983), contribute to an expanding number of years in which older people may be expected to remain economically and socially productive.

However, two factors call into question this picture of the elderly as an "untapped resource" of caring for kin and community. First, among women at least, there is some evidence that improved health and longevity may contribute to prolonged employment and not to increased unpaid care. While most of the increase in women's labor force participation over the past 30 years has been among middle-aged and younger women, employment among older women has also risen. Since 1960, part-time employment increased from 43 percent to 61 percent among women over 65 (U.S. Department of Health and Human Services, 1986). This suggests that some of this potential for extended productivity may be channeled into paid labor, and not unpaid services to family and friends. At the very least, it suggests that older women, as well as women in the middle, must juggle the competing demands of work and family care. It may be that those with greatest resources in terms of better health already have those resources tapped by participation in the paid labor force.

A second factor which may limit the involvement of the elderly in helping others is declining income. Since the majority of the elderly are women, and since two-thirds of elderly women have annual incomes of less than $15,000 (U.S. Bureau of the Census, 1988), increased reliance on the resources of the elderly may mean greater reliance on a population least able to bear the cost—at least the financial cost—of providing care.[3]

PERSPECTIVES ON OLDER PEOPLE GIVING CARE

Most previous research on caregiving by the elderly tends to focus on one of two areas: exchange of aid between generations or among friends and neighbors, or involvement in formal volunteer associations. Although this literature does little to assess the effects of age on care given across types of recipients, it provides some evidence of the ways in which age, as well as specific characteristics of the elderly, affect help given informally to family and friends and help given others through formal volunteer efforts.

Age and Giving Care

Two themes run throughout much of the study on aging. A great volume of research has focused on the interaction and integration of the elderly into networks of kin and friends. A second, more recent theme has been the care the elderly receive from kin—primarily adult daughters and daughters-in-law.

Although this literature does not examine caregiving by the elderly per se, it contains hints of the opportunities and obligations through which older people may become involved in helping others.

Aging research in the 1960s and early 1970s centered on dispelling the myth of the isolated elderly (Shanas, 1979a). By analyzing the number and frequency of contacts across generations, this research demonstrated that the transition to an industrialized economy did not result in the abandonment of the older generation (for a review of this literature, see Shanas, 1980).

At the same time, early aging research argued that, while not isolated, the elderly were engaged in shrinking networks of kin, friends, and voluntary associations (Babchuk and Booth 1969: Booth, 1972; Smith, 1966). The primary explanation for this process was that of psychological disengagement (Cath, 1972; Cumming and Henry, 1961). Disengagement theory argued that successful aging involved a gradual withdrawal from a broad range of social relations and obligations. Others, however, argued that the involvement of the elderly in networks of kin and volunteer associations was not monolithic, but rather affected by variation in work history (Maddox, 1966; Simpson and McKinney, 1966), socioeconomic class (Cumming, 1963; Maddox, 1972), and gender and residence (Rosow, 1967; Townsend, 1957). Thus, the concentration of available peers (in terms of homogeneity of marital status, gender, and age), higher income, and a more consistent history of employment were associated with greater and more persistent social interaction among the elderly.

Having demonstrated that disengagement was not an intrinsic, inevitable process that accompanied aging, the focus of more recent research has been on the types of aid and interaction the elderly *receive from* their kin. A rapidly expanding body of research has examined the ways in which age, family size, proximity, race, gender, and marriage affect the care the elderly receive (Babchuck et. al., 1979; Brody et al., 1984; Longino and Lipman, 1981; Matthews and Rosner, 1988; Spitze and Logan, 1989; Weeks and Cuellae, 1981). A primary focus has been the care the elderly receive from adult children (for an overview of this literature, see Horowitz, 1985b).

Together, studies done over the past three decades paint two, perhaps contradictory pictures of the involvement of the elderly in helping both families and communities. In one, while the elderly regularly interact with kin, they withdraw from broader social commitments and are primarily recipients of care. In the other, the elderly actively participate in well established patterns of help to both kith and kin. The reason for much of this divergence in perspectives is that most studies focus on a narrow range of help and support. Scattered studies have tried to address this issue by specifying not only the direction of intergenerational exchange and volunteer group participation, but the specific amount and types of support given (Morgan, 1982; Streib and Beck, 1980; Rossi and Rossi, 1990).

Rather than focusing on the ways in which the elderly withdraw from relationships with family and friends, much of this latter research focuses on the continuity of roles into old age. In doing so, it emphasizes the reconstruction and adaptation of previous roles in maintaining both independence and interdependence (Atchley, 1989; Rawlins, 1992). In terms of helping others, then, continuity theory suggests those who have been involved in giving care in the past tend to continue helping others into old age.

Taken together, previous research on aging and helping others raises three important issues. First, mixed findings reveal the importance of specifying not only total group membership or amount of support given to adult children, but also the types of groups and the range of help and support provided to both family and friends. Second, previous literature suggests that the disengagement of the elderly is selective and is not, perhaps, indicative of a general withdrawal from volunteer associations and relations with family and friends. Rather than examining either membership in volunteer groups or helping kin in isolation, it is important to link participation in volunteer associations with other sorts of giving care to family and friends. Third, continuity theory raises the question of the persistence of helping roles and, more specifically, the persistence of gender differences in helping others into old age.

Theories of Gender and Giving Care

Continuity theory, as well as theories of gender, would suggest that gender differences in giving care endure as men and women grow older. Influential work by Carol Gilligan (1982) argues that women develop a different morality than men. Women's morality is based on a sense of responsibility to particular others, while men's (and boy's) morality develops through their sense of individuality and the rights of others. Gilligan's work rests implicitly on earlier work by Chodorow (1974, 1978), whose critique of psychoanalytic theory argues that girls retain a greater sense of connectedness to others—a sense of connectedness that fulfills and reproduces women's assumption of primary responsibility for nurturing small children. By implication, then, women's early predominance in giving care is an expression of their ability to empathize and nurture—in short, to mother. These theorists might argue, then, that older women, like their younger counterparts, would be more likely than older men to nurture family and community because of their greater sense of connectedness and responsibility to care for others.

Yet many have argued that this perspective on gender masks important social-structural factors which shape women's and men's lives (Epstein, 1988). Rather than attributing gender differences in caring to differences in early social and psychological development, these theorists look to social, historical, and economic factors which shape gender roles. In particular, women's caregiving is rooted historically in the development of "separate spheres" that accompanied the rise of an industrial market economy (Smith-Rosenberg, 1975; Welter, 1966). Thus, while men moved into the paid labor force away from home, women—especially married women—stayed in the home. As part of this process, women's labor became focused on the unpaid work of child care and kinkeeping—their caring for those outside the home an extension of their caring for family inside the home. Thus, rather than a peculiar ethic of care among women, it is a historically based set of opportunities and alternatives that shapes the help men and women give others.[4]

To the extent that patterns of help are shaped by the differing demands of employment and family life, one might expect to find significant shifts in helping behaviors after retirement or widowhood. Perhaps men become more involved in helping kin after retirement and older women cut back on helping kin after being widowed. Physiological changes and changes in employment, in household composition and in the sex ratio of the population may all contribute to a convergence of gender roles as men and women age (Gutmann, 1985; Rossi, 1986). However, this question has been addressed in only a handful of studies, and these have produced somewhat conflicting results. While some researchers find that retirement has little impact on the help men give family (Aldous and Hulsman, 1986), others argue that relations with kin (which may or may not include giving care) increase as older people become less involved with their jobs (Schulman, 1975).

Although very few studies analyze the effects of retirement on the help older men and women give, a number examine the ways in which helping others is affected by employment. These suggest that employment affects helping behaviors differently for men and for women. For several years, researchers have argued that women's employment is more permeable to the demands of family care while men's family care is more permeable to the demands of employment (Pleck, 1977). Certainly, studies of men's and women's help to elderly parents fit this pattern.

A number of analyses show that employment does little to reduce gender differences in helping elderly parents. Regardless of whether or not they are employed, daughters provide more care to aging parents than do sons (Horowitz, 1985b). Others argue employed women may spend slightly less time caring for elderly parents than do homemakers (Lang and Brody, 1983). Yet research which specifies the types of care, as well as the amount of time spent helping parents finds that employed women substitute more money and paid services for hands-on services and labor-intensive care (Brody and Schoonover, 1986; Gerstel and Gallagher, 1990a). Thus employment influences giving care differently for men and for women—shaping the types and amount of help women provide, while having little effect on the help given by men.

Together, research on the impact of employment on gender differences in helping elderly parents and that on the effects of retirement on the help men give family suggest that gender differences in helping kin may not be solely due to the constraints of employment and family life. The same may be true for helping those outside the household—either friends, neighbors or others. Yet even fewer studies examine the help older people give friends; and none examines gender differences in the amount or types of help and support older men and women give to friends.

In contrast, previous research does, to a limited extent, address gender differences in volunteering. However, real differences in helping strangers are often obscured by differing or overinclusive definitions of volunteerism. In such research, membership in business associations, unions, and social clubs is often combined with membership in associations which provide help or support to the sick, poor, elderly or other groups of people in need. Also, participation is often measured solely in terms of number of memberships. Thus, level of involvement—in terms of hours of work, or specific tasks performed—is often omitted from the analysis.[5] As a result, discussion of gender differences in volunteering is inadequate, telling us very little about the effects of gender on help given others through formal volunteer associations.

A second difficulty is that most research does not focus specifically on volunteerism among the elderly. Still, studies of volunteerism within the general population consistently point to a slightly greater number of memberships among men than among women (Babchuk and Booth, 1969; Booth, 1972). Yet while men may belong to more volunteer groups, research indicates that women are more active than men in volunteer associations at every stage of the life cycle and that men's participation declines more rapidly with age than women's (Babchuk and Booth, 1969; Chambre, 1984; Hausknecht, 1962). As with helping kin, these findings suggest that men's volunteerism may also be linked to their employment; while women's volunteerism is more an extension of their involvement in child rearing and kinkeeping.

Theories of Marriage and Giving Care

There is some evidence, then, that suggests the help older men and women give may be linked to their roles as breadwinners and homemakers, at the same time that gender differences in giving care may also reflect a greater ethic of care among women. For women in particular, there is reason to believe marriage is an especially salient factor in affecting giving care, just as it is pivotal to the organization of women's domestic and family roles.

At the same time, however, the effects of marriage on the help women give may be somewhat contradictory. On the one hand, marriage integrates women—whether into larger networks of family or friends or into couples oriented volunteer associations (Fischer, 1982; O'Donnell, 1985). In doing so, marriage may expand older women's opportunities for helping others—be they family, friends or others.   On the other hand, marriage is also "greedy"—in that it focuses women's time and energy on caring for those inside the nuclear family, while limiting opportunities and resources for helping others (Coser and Coser, 1974; Gerstel, 1988). Marriage, then, may have profound consequences for older women's giving care—both in expanding care to kin (adult children in particular) and in limiting care to nonkin.

NOTES

1. In this context, recent concern over the demise of the family and the community may be intensified by the perception that the demands of an industrial economy not only threaten particular family and community forms but are essentially dehumanizing.

2. Between 1982 and 1987, 105,000 new service organizations were begun (Independent Sector, 1988)--suggesting that the private volunteer sector may be responding to decreased federal spending on social welfare programs.

3. It should be noted that limiting discussions of giving care to financial assistance severely underestimates the kind, the range, as well as the amount of help actually performed. According to the Independent Sector's survey, "Giving and Volunteering in the United States" (1988), $51 million was given to charities in 1988. For the same year, this survey also estimates that value of time and services given to private charities was worth nearly $150 billion. According to these figures, unpaid services have nearly three times the value of financial contributions to charity.

4. Recently, a number of theorists have begun to argue that women's predominance in helping others reflects a female "ethic of care" that ought to be expanded to society as a whole (see, for example, Baire, 1985; Held, 1987; Ruddick, 1984). Interestingly, these arguments echo those of feminists a century ago who claimed that women's superior morality ought to be extended beyond the home into movements for social and moral reform.

5. This is the case in two of the most comprehensive national surveys on volunteering, the General Social Survey and the Survey on Giving and Volunteering.

2

Study Design and Methodology

INTRODUCTION

This study is based on in-depth personal interviews with a stratified sample of 324 women and men, age 25 to 94. Although time consuming, this type of interview allowed deeper exploration of key issues than would have been possible with either a telephone or a mail survey. The sample was limited to the household population of blacks and whites living in Springfield, Massachusetts.[1] The research took place in two phases. The first focused on married women age 25 to 70 and approximately half of their husbands. These women were stratified by employment and race: approximately a third were employed full time, a third employed part time, and a third not working for pay.[2] About 11.6 percent were black—only slightly lower than the national average of 12 percent (U.S. Bureau of the Census, 1992). A total of 241 respondents were interviewed during the first phase of the research, with a response rate of 60 percent.

The second phase of the research extended the original sample to include married women over 70, approximately half of their husbands, and widows age 60 and older. Eighty-three additional interviews were conducted during this phase of the research. The sampling procedure and interviews were identical for all respondents. This study primarily focuses on a subset of respondents— married women and men, and widowed women, all age 60 or older (N=135). The chapters on gender (Part II) focus on married men and women age 60 and older (N=87) while the chapters on marriage and giving care (Part III) focus on married and widowed women age 60 and older (N=106).

SAMPLING PROCEDURE

Respondents were selected by using a random sample of telephone numbers from the most recent telephone directory. Each number was dialed a minimum because of nonresponse and replaced with another number. Each was asked whether there were any women over the age of 25 presently living in that household. If such a person lived there, interviewers asked to speak to that woman, using a random selection procedure to select a respondent if there were more than one woman over 25. Potential respondents were also screened for marital status (either married or widowed and 60 or older), race (either black or white), and employment status (employed full time, employed part time or working as homemakers).

Those who fit the sampling criteria were asked to volunteer to participate in a household interview of community life being conducted under the auspices of the University of Massachusetts at Amherst. Some women were hesitant to participate in a household interview—citing lack of interest or fear as the reason for refusal. In these cases, women were asked whether they would accept a letter (see the Appendix) explaining more about the study, and a second contact the following week. Almost all agreed. Early in the second phase of this research (that focusing on married women and men over 70 and widows over 60), an alarmingly high proportion of the women refused to participate in the study.[3] Rather than continuing to contact these elderly respondents a second time by telephone, I went to their homes and asked potential respondents directly what would be a convenient time to do an interview. This strategy worked remarkably well—the majority of respondents agreed to be interviewed at the time of the drop-in, while others scheduled (and all but two kept) appointments for a later date. The overall acceptance rate among the elderly was 62 percent, which compares favorably with other studies involving household interviews with random samples of older persons (e.g., see Aldous, 1987; Anderson, 1984; Greenberg and Becker, 1988).

In order to capture the "his and hers" marriage (Bernard, 1972), husbands and wives were interviewed separately. At the completion of a wife's interview, she was asked what would be a good time to contact her husband about participating in the study. Slightly less than one third of the wives (29.6 percent) refused to allow the interviewer to ask their husbands to do an interview. The most frequently cited reason was that they believed their husbands were "too busy" or "wouldn't be interested." Approximately one third of the husbands whose wives refused an interview for them were employed either full time or part time. The majority, however were retired.[4] Other women refused because they believed their husbands unable to do an interview because of some disabling physical or mental condition.[5]

Of those husbands who were asked to do an interview, 82 percent agreed.[6] The final sample of respondents age 60 and older comprised 51 widows, 55 married women and 32 of their husbands (Table 2.1). The mean age for women was 71, and for men 68.

Interviews consisted of both closed-ended and open-ended questions and lasted an average of 1 hour and 15 minutes — ranging from 30 minutes to more

Table 2.1
Distribution of Respondents
by Age, Gender and Marital Status

	Number	Percent	Mean Age
I. Total Sample	324	100.0	52.63
Men	94	29.0	49.12
Women	230	71.0	54.07
Married	179	77.8	48.14
Widowed	51	22.2	74.88
II. Older Sample	138	100.0	70.39
Men	32	23.2	68.31
Women	106	76.8	71.02
Married	55	51.9	67.44
Widowed	51	48.1	74.88
III. Younger Sample	186	100.0	39.46
Men	62	33.3	39.21
Women	124	66.7	39.58

Notes: The older sample comprises respondents age 60+, the younger all respondents age 25 to 59.

than 3 hours. In most cases, these interviews occurred in the respondent's home. A few respondents asked that they be interviewed at work and one woman requested to be interviewed at the place where she was volunteering.

Each interview began with the administration of a closed-ended questionnaire.[7] Women frequently offered comments or initiated discussion in response to issues raised in the questionnaire. In the second part of each interview, individually tailored probes served as a follow-up to the quantitative items. Women were asked to describe in detail the history and motivation of their giving care and its relation to their employment and family histories.

Discussions were tape-recorded, and all recordings and interview notes were transcribed.

MEASUREMENT

The questionnaire contained items constructed to assess the amount, types, and range of care that respondents provide informally to family, friends and neighbors, as well as help given others through formal volunteer efforts. In addition, we assessed a range of sociodemographic variables, and several series of questions assessed the objective and subjective consequences of women's and men's caregiving, as well as attitudes toward the public and private provision of care.

Informal Help to Family and Friends

In order to capture the range and extent of help given by the elderly, the questionnaire used a technique adapted from Fischer (1982) for network analysis. Although Fischer developed this technique to assess help received, it was adapted for this analysis to assess care given.

Each respondent was given a list of tasks and asked whether in the last month he or she had provided any of these types of help and support to parents. This process was repeated for parents-in-law, adult children, other relatives, and friends and neighbors. The types of help listed fell into three general categories: practical help, personal help, and material help. The types of practical help were the following: prepared a meal or brought food, did laundry, repaired things, gave a ride, helped someone who was sick or disabled, did banking or helped with finance, took care of a child, or did cleaning or other household chores, or other help.[8] The following were the types of personal help listed: discussed personal problems or concerns, gave information about where to find work or talked to employer for them, and gave other advice such as where to find social services or help with a bureaucracy. The types of material help listed were the following: gave or lent money, gave a gift, and gave or lent goods—either new or used. Respondents were prompted to mention *any* help or support they had given, "whether major or minor, over the phone or in person, during a visit."[9]

A list was made of the first names of each person mentioned. This list was shown to the respondent, and he or she was asked whether there was anyone else he or she helped last month, the type of help given, and whether there was anyone not on the list who had helped the respondent in the previous month. These additional names were added to the list.

Many respondents had difficulty recalling the types of help and support they had given family and friends during the previous month. Some insisted that they had not done anything for anyone, and only after repeated prompting began to recall the often substantial help they had given others in the previous month. Again and again, respondents would begin by saying, "Well, I did something for (some person), but that doesn't really count" or "It wasn't anything, really." This reticence to acknowledge or even recognize help given, particularly among wives and widows, illustrates the hidden nature of much caregiving and may, as other work suggests, reflect a more general tendency among women to devalue the work that they do (Daniels, 1985).

In order to facilitate respondents' recall, each was prompted to think of everyday kinds of help—minor or major, over the phone or in person, emotional, material, as well as physical help—as they considered what they might have done for each category of persons (aging parents or in-laws, adult children, other relatives, and friends and neighbors). Once assured that it was precisely these everyday tasks that were of interest, many respondents explained in detail the many and varied types of help in which they had been involved.

After completing the list of persons helped, each respondent was asked a series of questions about each person named: age, sex, geographic proximity, marital status, financial status, degree of intimacy, whether or not he or she had similar religion, race, or health; and whether or not the person named was receiving any public assistance other than Social Security. By gathering information on those to whom care was given, characteristics of the caregiver may be analyzed in conjunction with those of the recipients.

In addition, long-term involvement in giving care was assessed by asking respondents whether they had *ever* housed anyone for a significant length of time (more than a week), given anyone a significant amount of money (either a loan or a gift), or cared for anyone who was seriously ill. Respondents were urged to consider anyone (family, friend or stranger) to whom they had provided these forms of care. The number of people to whom respondents had given significant help in the past is an indicator of their history of giving care. Since previous research argues that older volunteers are volunteers who have aged (Chambre, 1984), this measure provides an estimate of a broad range of helping behaviors across the life course and may be interpreted as a rough measure of the degree to which each may be characterized as a "caregiver."

Helping Others through Formal Volunteerism

After assessing help given to family and friends, respondents were asked about their participation in both formal and informal volunteer associations. The questionnaire used an adaptation of the aided recall technique developed by C. N. Bull at the Institute for Social Research at the University of Michigan in 1952

(Bull, 1982). This technique was adapted by Babchuk and Booth (1969) and has been used in other research to elicit detailed information about group membership and participation (Booth 1972; McPherson and Smith-Lovin, 1982). Rather than presenting respondents with a long list of organizations and asking them to indicate the ones to which they currently belong (as is done in the General Social Survey), aided recall prompts respondents to think about a number of different categories of groups, and to indicate whether they currently belong to or do any work with groups like these. Thus, respondents were asked about involvement in 9 different types of groups: charity and welfare organizations, youth related groups, job related groups such as a union or a professional association, veterans or patriotic organizations, organizations for the elderly, political or public interest groups, ethnic or national groups, fraternal or service organizations, and church or temple related groups.

If respondents indicated that they were currently involved in a particular type of group, they were asked to name the specific group to which they belonged. As with persons helped, interviewers made a list of group memberships. Each person was shown the list, and asked whether there were any *other* groups— large or small, formal or informal—that they currently belonged to or did work with that were not on the list.[10]

As with the list of persons helped, respondents were also asked a series of questions about the characteristics of their group memberships: frequency of attending meetings; hours of work a year; amount of gifts and contributions (both monetary and material contributions); length of membership; whether each group were local, regional, national or international; and whether their participation in each group had provided help to the poor, sick, elderly or other groups of people in need.

More detailed information was gathered on the kinds of tasks performed for groups for which a respondent performed 50 or more hours of service a month. For these high involvement groups, respondents were handed a list of group tasks and asked whether in the last month they had done any of these tasks for each organization with which they were heavily involved.[11]

Finally, involvement in helping others was assessed by asking each respondent whether, in the past year, he or she had done any other kind of charity or volunteer work—helping the elderly, the sick, the poor or any other people in need who were not relatives or friends—and if so, how many hours he or she had spent doing that work. An estimate of total formal help was then obtained by combining these two measures: hours of participation in volunteer groups and other hours of charity work.

Sociodemographic Variables

Along with these detailed measures of family and community care, data were also collected on sociodemographic characteristics: age, sex, household composition, employment status (both current and past), income, education, religion and religious activity, and length of residence in Springfield. The form of many of these items was taken from the General Social Survey.

Health. Three measures of general physical health and capacities were included in the questionnaire. First, was the respondent's self-rating of general physical health as excellent, good, fair, poor or very poor.[12] Second, using the same scale, the interviewer rated each respondent's general physical condition. This measure replicated and provided a comparison with respondent's self-rating. Third, a modified form of the Instrumental Activities of Daily Living Scale (IADL) was administered to each respondent over 60. This scale, developed by Lawton and Brody (1969), and is widely used to assess physical capacities (Stone, Cafferata and Sangl, 1987).[13] The respondent's self-rating and two scales based on the IADL were highly correlated with each other (r=.44, p≤.001). Since the greatest number of cases was available for self-reported health, that measure was used in this analysis.

Employment. Respondents were asked whether they were employed, retired or homemakers, as well as the number of hours they actually worked for pay the previous week. Including multiple measures of employment proved significant since both homemakers and retired women and men often identified themselves as unemployed, whereas they were actually doing (or still doing) some work for pay.[14] Both primary identity and actual work patterns were captured by using these alternative measures of employment.

SAMPLE COMPARABILITY

Although the sample of elderly used in this study was relatively small, on a number of key sociodemographic characteristics it compares favorably with census data for the nation as a whole (Table 2.2). Mean family income for older respondents interviewed between 1987 and 1989 was $21,417, compared with a national average of $20,383 among those age 60 and older in 1987. The percentage of those still employed is also similar for the older Springfield sample and the nation (27.5 percent compared with 22.8 percent).

Where the older Springfield sample differs from the nation as a whole is in level of education and race. Overall, the men and women interviewed in Springfield were more highly educated than their national counterparts. Almost 72 percent of the older Springfield sample received a high school diploma or higher degree; compared with 56.9 percent of those 60 and older for the nation

Table 2.2
Comparison of Older Sample Characteristics
with National Data for Men and Women Age 60+

	Springfield Sample	National Data[a]
Employment (%)	27.5 %	22.8 %
High School Education[b]	71.7 %	56.9 %
Income[c]	$ 21,471	$ 20,383
Race (% Blacks)	18.1 %	8.9 %

[a] Source for national figures: U.S. Bureau of the Census, Statistical Abstracts, 1992.
[b] Percent who have received a high school diploma or higher degree.
[c] Annual family income, 1988.

as a whole.[15] Finally, 18.9 percent of the older Springfield sample were black, compared with 8.9 percent among those 60 and older on the national level. This reflects a purposeful oversampling of blacks in order to have a large enough sample for statistical analysis.

NOTES

1. Because of the limited sample size and the linguistic ability of the interviewers, those who were neither black nor white, never married, cohabiting, separated or divorced were excluded from the sample.

2. Approximately a third (37.5 percent) of the women who identified themselves as homemakers over the phone were actually working part time—often at home—doing typing or piecework. The same was true of retired men in the second phase of the research—approximately a third (33.5 percent) of the men who identified themselves as retired actually did some work for pay, often as consultants or occasional workers. Because of the interest in the effects of employment on giving care, all of these respondents were asked questions for both employed and nonemployed.

3. Nine of the first fifteen women recontacted by telephone refused to participate even after receiving a letter introducing the study—a refusal rate of 60 percent.

4. Approximately 25 percent of the husbands whose wives refused for them were working full time, 14 percent were working part time, and 60 percent were retired. Among younger respondents (age 25 to 59) only 12.5 percent of the wives refused for their husbands to be asked to do an interview, and all of these men were employed full time or temporarily out of work.

5. Only 3 or 4 wives refused to let their husbands be interviewed on the grounds of ill health. Even though this number was small, the estimates of help given by elderly married men may slightly overestimate actual helping behaviors within the population as a whole. Similar refusal rates on the grounds of ill health have been found in other research on random samples of the elderly (Anderson, 1984).

6. While we do not have information on women who refused to be interviewed, it is possible to compare wives of men who were interviewed with wives of men who were not interviewed. On almost all important characteristics, these two groups do not significantly differ. There is no difference on demographic variables such as race, age, personal income, employment (yes/no), or occupation (professional/managerial versus other). Family income does significantly differ for these two groups, but only at the $p \leq .10$ level. Women whose husbands were interviewed had a mean family income of $40,000, while women whose husbands were not interviewed had a family income of $36,000. It is important to note that there are no significant differences between wives of respondent husbands and wives of nonrespondent husbands on any of the measures of help and support.

7. The questionnaire was originally developed by Naomi Gerstel for use in her study "Women and the Transformation of Gender Roles," funded by the Rockefeller Foundation and conducted at the University of Massachusetts between September 1988 and November 1989.

8. The large majority of "other" tasks entailed 4 similar kinds of help. These were coded for analysis as watching a home while someone was away, visiting someone who was sick, doing yard work, and helping someone move.

9. Some scholars have argued that ties to kin may be underestimated when technological enhancements to support (such as the telephone) are omitted (Litwak and Kulis, 1987). While this study did not include a specific measure of telephone contact, many respondents specified the telephone as a significant means of providing emotional support or advice.

10. The majority of these additional groups were recoded into the group categories already listed. Those groups which did not fall into one of the original 9 group types were coded into four additional categories: recreational, hobby or social groups; neighborhood or community upkeep groups (e.g. Crime Watch); arts and cultural groups (e.g. Friends of Springfield Library); and other groups.

11. These group tasks were as follows: provided direct care to other people, acted as bookkeeper or treasurer, supervised or coordinated other volunteers, raised money, organized group meetings, acted as spokesperson for the group, presided over group meetings, wrote letters or reports on behalf of the group, recruited new members, took minutes, typed or did other secretarial jobs, or made or received phone calls on behalf of the group.

12. For the purposes of this study, it was assumed that a respondent's subjective evaluation of his or her general health was an adequate measure for assessing the effects of health on involvement in family and community caregiving. While subjective evaluations of health are not always consistent with actual health status (Schaie, 1988), and while elderly persons are generally more pessimistic about their overall health than are middle aged persons (Leukoff, Cleary and Wetle, 1987), what is of interest here—given the length of the interview and limited resources—is how perceived health status, and not acutal physical condition, affects giving care. In addition, this single item measure ("Would you say your physical health in general is excellent, good, fair, poor or very poor?") has been shown to be stable in a variety of situations and studies (Shanas, 1977; Stahl, 1984).

13. The IADL includes items on the degree of independence in preparing meals, doing housework, doing laundry, shopping, taking medications, getting around outside, managing transportation, using the telephone, and managing one's own finances. As such, it provides a third indicator for assessing the degree to which physical condition affects giving care.

14. See note 2.

15. A number of respondents told me that Springfield had one of the best school systems in the nation. In fact, several said they had moved to Springfield specifically because of the reputation of its school system. This may contribute to the high percentage of those with a high school degree or better within the Springfield sample.

3

Age and Giving Care

There was a period when I couldn't say no, but I can now. When you get to my age you can do what you want.

72 year-old married woman

INTRODUCTION

Two very different images of the elderly emerge from research on aging and recent trends in public policy and employment. On the one hand, the elderly are often seen as a potential social problem—as mainly recipients rather than providers of care. Shrinking family size and high mobility of kin and neighbors have prompted concern that increasing numbers of older people—mostly widows—finish their lives in loneliness and isolation. In spite of two decades of research, the myth of the isolated elderly remains a frequent theme in aging research (Shanas, 1979a). More recently, concern over the financial and emotional costs involved in caring for aging parents has shifted the emphasis toward research on caregivers to the dependent elderly (Abel, 1991; Schulz et al., 1990; Stone, Cafferata and Sangl, 1987). The large majority of these caregivers are women (Horowitz, 1985b)—many of whom are caught not only "in the middle" of two generations needing care (Brody, 1990) but in the middle of employment and family as well (Scharlach and Boyd, 1989; Stoller and Pugliesi, 1989). Neither image of the elderly—as isolated or as dependent recipients of care—is particularly appealing.

In dramatic contrast to these images of the elderly as either isolated from family and friends or frail and dependent is the profile of the healthy and involved elderly volunteer. These are the new volunteers illustrated in a recent television commercial by the retired, and now loved, IRS agent who volunteers to help those struggling to complete their tax forms. Yet, we know very little about the help older people give others through formal volunteerism, or how volunteerism affects informal help to family and friends.

PERSPECTIVES ON AGING

Contrasting images of the elderly as either isolated and alone or active volunteers reflect two larger theoretical perspectives on aging. The first, coming out of research on intergenerational relations, argues that while not isolated, the elderly are involved in shrinking networks of kin, friends and voluntary associations (Booth, 1972; Smith, 1966). The primary explanation for this process is that of psychological disengagement (Cumming and Henry, 1961). Although the process of disengagement may be affected by a number of social characteristics (Maddox, 1972; Rosow, 1967; Townsend, 1957), the theory generally argues that successful aging involves a gradual withdrawal from a range of social relations and obligations.

Rather than focusing on the ways in which the elderly disengage from relations with family and friends, more recent research focuses on the continuity of roles into old age. In doing so, it emphasizes the active reconstruction and adaptation of previous roles in maintaining both independence and interdependence (Atchley, 1989; Payne and Bull, 1985). From this perspective, those who have been involved in helping others in the past tend to continue helping others in old age. This supports the image of the healthy and involved older volunteer. Yet there is some evidence that continuity in giving care may vary depending on whether we are considering helping adult children, other relatives, friends and neighbors, or strangers in the community.

Age and Help to Adult Children

Although much early research focuses on the frequency of interaction and the amount of aid adult children provide aging parents, some argue that a greater proportion of older persons give, rather than receive, help from adult children; and that greater quantities of help flow from parent to child than from adult child to parent (Hill, 1970; Streib, 1965). More recent research has begun to specify the types of aid parents give adult children (see reviews by Morgan, 1982; Streib and Beck, 1980). Parents provide significant emotional support and advice in times of difficulty such as divorce (Hagestad, 1982; Hetherington, Cox and Cox, 1982; C. L. Johnson, 1988; Tinsley and Parke, 1984) and widowhood (Bankoff, 1984; Greenberg and Becker, 1988), as well as housing during periods of transition (DeVanzo and Goldscheider, 1990). Parental help is not confined to times of personal distress. A number of studies argue that parents routinely provide practical, personal and material help to adult children (Antonucci and Akiyama, 1987; Brody, 1985; Rossi and Rossi, 1990; Spitze and Logan, 1992). The types of support provided, however, may change as parents age. In particular, financial assistance and practical support may decline less dramatically over time than does either personal support or gifts of goods (Cheal, 1988; Rossi and Rossi, 1990).

Age and Helping Other Relatives

Although more limited, a few studies suggest that the elderly also provide a range of help and support to relatives other than adult children. Grandmothers play a significant role in providing support for child rearing, particularly among urban blacks (Malson, 1983; Stack, 1974). Beyond "backup babysitter," grandparents also serve as confidants to adolescent grandchildren (Bengtson, 1985; Robertson, 1977), give gifts of money and goods (Wood and Robertson, 1978), and provide transportation as well as other practical help and support (Gladstone, 1988; Wood and Robertson, 1978). Older men and women also provide significant personal support to siblings (McGhee, 1985; O'Bryant, 1988)—support that may increase, rather than decline, over the life cycle (Goetting, 1986). Taken together, these findings suggest that helping kin may be characterized by the continuity of caring roles into old age, as well as a shift in the types of care provided.

Age and Help to Friends and Neighbors

Most analyses of adult relations with friends and neighbors focus on frequency of interaction, not giving care. Townsend (1957), in his classic study of aging and family life, argued that interaction with friends declines with age. To the extent that help is given within the context of some interaction, we would expect older people to be less involved in helping friends than younger adults. Yet others argue that casual relations with friends increase, rather than decline, with age (Fischer, 1982; Hochschild, 1973). To the extent that this is the case, it may be that older people spend less time helping friends, but help a larger number of casual friends overall than do younger adults.

Age and Volunteerism

Finally, scattered research suggests that both persistence and change may characterize the help older people give others through formal volunteer efforts. While some early studies of disengagement from volunteer associations found group membership declined with age (Foskett, 1955; Scott, 1957), others found very little decline in membership, except among the very old (Booth, 1972). Still others suggested that volunteerism is class-related—gradually increasing with age among upper class men (Bell and Force, 1956; Beyer and Woods,

1963), and decreasing most dramatically among the poor and the working class (ACTION, 1975; Babchuk and Booth, 1969).

These divergent findings may be a consequence of the measures used in assessing volunteerism—some studies focusing on membership and others on hours of participation. Both are, of course, important depending on whether the interest is in breadth or depth of involvement. This study assesses both the number of groups to which people belong and the amount of time they spend volunteering. Moreover, respondents were also asked about the specific types of volunteer associations to which they belong and the types of needy who receive help and support through their volunteer efforts. Thus, we examine not only the breadth, but also something of the depth and variety of older people's involvement in helping those who are neither family nor friends.

HYPOTHESES

Together, findings from previous research suggest several hypotheses about the ways in which age may affect patterns of help to family, friends and others. Declining material and physical resources, coupled with strong normative obligations to help those who are more closely related (Rossi and Rossi, 1990), may mean that age has less effect on informal help to kin—particularly adult children—than on help to friends and neighbors. To the extent that behavior follows normative expectations to provide care, we might expect younger adults to help more kin and more friends than do older adults. This difference between older and younger adults, however, ought to be smaller for kin than it is for friends. Similarly, we would expect smaller age differences in hours of care to kin than to nonkin (both friends and neighbors, and strangers in the community).

Second, previous research suggests that age may affect the types of care provided. While the elderly presumably have more time to devote to caring for family and friends, they also experience a range of declining resources on which they can draw in helping others. Yet, declining financial or physical resources may be counterbalanced by fewer competing demands from work and family obligations. Because this analysis includes ordinary as well as extraordinary personal help and support (everyday talk about personal problems and concerns along with comfort or advice in times of crisis, for example), we might expect to find less difference between younger and older adults in personal help than in either practical or material help and support. Furthermore, we might expect greater differences between older and younger adults in material help and support, especially that given to friends.

Third, previous research suggests that age may also affect help given others through formal volunteer efforts. These effects may vary, however, depending on the dimension of volunteerism being considered. Along with number of group memberships, this study examines age differences in hours of participation, specific types of groups, and the types of needy helped through volunteer efforts. I expect that group membership significantly differs for older and younger adults—most dramatically for groups whose functions are closely related to position in the life course (e.g., youth groups or groups that assist the elderly). More importantly, given the implications of public policy encouraging greater volunteerism among the elderly, this chapter assesses age differences in volunteerism that helps the needy and tests the hypothesis that age has less effect on the amount of time devoted to volunteering, particularly volunteering to help those in need.

ANALYSIS

The analysis that follows compares patterns of help among older and younger respondents. The younger sample includes men and women age 24 to 59 (N=186). The older sample includes men and women age 60 and older (N=138). Because the data are cross-sectional, not longitudinal, the analysis cannot examine either cohort effects or the process of aging itself. Instead, it focuses on current differences in giving care between two groups of adults: one younger and middle aged, the other the aging and very old. Doing so provides a comparative framework within which important differences in men's and women's help to different types of recipients may be explored.

Age and Giving Care

Table 3.1 presents a comparison of three dimensions of help for older and younger adults. These are whether or not any help was given in the previous month, the number of each category of recipients to whom care was given, and the amount of time spent providing that care. At the simplest level, we find older adults are significantly less likely to help each category of recipients than are their younger counterparts. This is the case across types of recipients, regardless of whether we are considering informal help to any person (94 versus 99 percent), help to kin (89 versus 98 percent), or help to friends (67 versus 87 percent). The same is true for participation in formal volunteer efforts. Older men and women are significantly less likely to belong to volunteer groups or to volunteer than are their younger counterparts (64 versus 74 percent).

Although a greater percentage of younger adults give help, the large majority of the elderly *are* involved in helping family, friends and others. In fact, approximately 90 percent of the older sample helped at least one person or at least one relative in the month prior to the interview. Although somewhat less, the majority were also involved in giving some sort of help to friends, as well

Table 3.1
Age and Informal Help to Family, Friends and Neighbors
(t-Tests)

I. % Who Helped Any	Young Adults	Old
Person	.99 (.07)	.94 (.24)*
Kin[a]	.98 (.15)	.89 (.31)*
Adult children[b]	.95 (.22)	.82 (.38)**
Other relatives[c]	.96 (.19)	.71 (.04)***
Friends	.87 (.34)	.67 (.47)***
Groups	.74 (.440	.64 (.48)*
II. Number Helped		
Total Persons	8.53 (5.08)	5.96 (4.49)***
Kin[a]	4.93 (2.71)	3.82 (3.12)***
Adult children[b]	2.16 (1.32)	2.13 (1.78)
Other relatives[c]	4.22 (2.73)	1.97 (2.36)***
Friends	3.59 (3.45)	2.14 (2.29)***
Groups	2.32 (2.69)	2.23 (2.48)
III. Mean Hours Helping per Month		
Total Persons	41.84 (46.11)	42.02 (55.88)
Kin[a]	30.85 (42.07)	34.31 (53.10)
Adult children[b]	34.57 (47.10)	26.46 (49.50)
Other relatives[c]	19.57 (28.20)	11.49 (20.20)**
Friends	10.99 (14.30)	7.71 (14.37)*
Groups	7.45 (11.53)	9.94 (17.20)+

Notes: The symbols indicate 1-tailed test for significance: +≤.10; *≤.05; **≤.01; ***≤.001. Standard deviations are in parentheses. Younger, N=186. Older=138. [a] Includes adult children, parents, parents-in-law, siblings, etc..
[b] Children age 18 and older. [c] Relatives other than adult children.

as strangers. In terms of contact with others in which older people provide help (rather than simply receive it) the large majority of elderly are clearly not isolated and alone.

Older people also help fewer people overall than do younger and middle aged adults (5.96 versus 8.53 people). They help significantly fewer kin overall (3.82 versus 4.93 kin), as well as fewer relatives other than adult children (1.97 versus 4.22 other relatives) and fewer friends (2.14 versus 3.59 friends). However, older and younger adults do not significantly differ in helping adult children. Comparing only those who are parents of adult children, both older and younger adults help approximately two adult children—giving some indication that parental care persists into old age.

In the breadth of help to those who are most closely related, then, the old and the young do not significantly differ. A somewhat different picture emerges when we look at depth, or hours, of care. Older and younger parents of adult children do not significantly differ in the amount of time they spend helping their children (26.5 versus 34.6 hours per month). Yet older people spend significantly less time helping other relatives (11.5 versus 19.6 hours), as well as significantly less time helping friends (7.7 versus 11 hours), than do their younger counterparts. In terms of the depth of care, then, these data provide some support for the hypothesis that older adults withdraw from more extensive helping relations "into the family."

This image of withdrawal is not supported, however, by the data on help to those who are neither kin nor friends. Older and younger people do not significantly differ on our first measure of volunteerism: number of group memberships. Both older and younger adults belong to a similar number of volunteer groups (2.32). Nor do they significantly differ in the depth, or hours, of involvement in volunteer associations overall: both spend approximately 42 hours per month volunteering. However, when we consider only volunteer activities through which some sort of help was given, we find older adults spend significantly more time than younger adults helping the needy (9.9 versus 7.5 hours per month)—suggesting that withdrawal from social relations, especially those involving giving care, is selective, to the extent that it occurs at all.

Types of Informal Care to Family and Friends

Table 3.2 compares the types of support older and younger adults provide informally to kin and to friends. Both older and younger adults provide more of each type of help—whether practical, personal or material—to kin than they do to friends. In fact, both perform approximately twice the number of tasks, across types of support, for kin as for friends. Clearly, patterns of help exist (and appear to persist) in which helping kin takes precedence over helping friends and neighbors.

Table 3.2
Types of Informal Help Given to Kin and Friends by Age of Caregiver
(t-Tests)

Type of Help[a]	Help to Kin			Help to Friends		
	Young	Old	Difference	Young	Old	Difference
Practical	5.20 (4.88)	3.75 (3.75) **	28%	2.43 (2.90)	1.26 (2.56) ***	48%
Personal	4.23 (3.19)	2.17 (2.53) ***	49%	2.47 (3.18)	.80 (1.46) ***	68%
Material	3.96 (3.56)	2.31 (2.87) ***	42%	1.35 (2.33)	.78 (1.56) **	42%

Notes: Symbols indicate one-tailed test for significance between younger and older adults, based on a separate variance estimate: $+\leq.10$; $*\leq.05$; $**\leq.01$; $***\leq.001$. Standard deviations in parentheses. Young, N=186. Old, N=138.
[a] Total number of practical, personal, or material tasks performed in the previous month.

Contrary to the hypothesis that older and younger adults differ most greatly in providing material support, the data in Table 3.2 suggest older and younger adults differ most in the total number of personal tasks they do for either kin or friends. Older men and women give half as much personal support to kin as do younger adults, compared with 28 percent as much practical support and 42 percent as much material support given to kin. Similarly, older men and women give 68 percent as much personal help to friends as do younger adults; compared with 48 percent as much practical help and 42 percent as much material support. In terms of types of support, these data substantiate the notion that age depresses older people's help to people they know. Because the largest difference between younger and older people is in providing personal help and support, it may be that material and physical resources are less important in shaping patterns of care among the elderly than is having less emotional energy for giving care.

Age and Types of Formal Volunteerism

In terms of volunteerism, group membership tends to be closely related to position in the life course (Table 3.3). Older men and women belong to significantly more veterans groups, groups for the elderly, service groups, and recreational groups than do younger adults. In contrast, younger adults belong to more youth related groups and more job oriented groups. Younger adults also belong to slightly more political and ethnic groups than their older counterparts (p≤.10). No significant differences exist, however, in the number of welfare, religious, community or cultural groups to which older and younger adults belong. Thus, while the types of groups to which older adults belong may shift

Table 3.3
Types of Groups by Age of Participant
(t-Tests)

Type of Group Helped (#)	Young (N=186)	Old (N=138)
Welfare	.17 (.78)	.26 (.71)
Youth	.37 (.69)	.07 (.25)***
Job	.56 (.95)	.15 (.67)***
Veterans	.03 (.21)	.14 (.50)**
Elderly	.04 (.19)	.59 (.72)***
Political	.37 (.99)	.20 (.86)+
Ethnic	.11 (.39)	.06 (.24)+
Service	.05 (.24)	.12 (.34)*
Religious	.47 (.87)	.44 (.80)
Recreational	.08 (.37)	.14 (.44)+
Community	.02 (.13)	.02 (.15)
Art/Cultural	.04 (.20)	.06 (.29)

Notes: Symbols indicate one-tailed test for significance based on a separate variance estimate: +≤.10; *≤.05; **≤.01; ***≤.001. Standard deviations in parentheses.

as age related interests change, overall participation appears to be relatively stable into old age.

More important perhaps, given the recent state interest in promoting volunteerism among the elderly, is the degree to which this participation results in help and support to those in need who are neither kin nor friends. Table 3.4 compares the percent who help with the amount of time older and younger adults spend in volunteer activities which help the sick, poor, elderly or other needy.

Table 3.4
Charity Work by Age
(t-Tests)

I. % Who Volunteer to Help	Young	Old
The Poor	.52 (1.05)	.52 (1.17)
The Sick	.44 (.94)	.59 (1.10)
The Elderly	.41 (.91)	.60 (1.15)*
Other Needy	.62 (1.17)	.57 (1.34)
Any Type of Needy People[a]	1.05 (1.76)	1.06 (1.57)
II. Hours Helping		
The Poor	33.83 (93.15)	48.82 (133.75)
The Sick	29.32 (86.24)	53.46 (130.60)*
The Elderly	27.47 (82.85)	56.46 (136.12)**
Other Needy	40.25 (97.85)	59.36 (157.84)
Any Type of Needy People[b]	50.04 (106.00)	84.31 (189.64)*
III. Total Hours Charity Work[c]	4.14 (8.81)	6.82 (14.95)*
IV. Proportion of Volunteering Devoted to Charity Work	.31 (.41)	.32 (.43)

Notes: Level of significance: $+\leq.10$; $*\leq.05$; $**\leq.01$; $***\leq.001$. Standard deviations in parentheses. Young, N=186. Old, N=138. [a] Since each group may help more than one type of needy person, mean scores may be greater than 1.
[b] Hours spent the previous year helping each group of needy persons may overlap (e.g., hours to poor may also have been hours to the sick).
[c] Hours of charity work per month.

Overall, older men and women are more likely to help those in need through volunteer group efforts than are their younger counterparts. Slightly more than half (between 52 and 60 percent) of all groups to which the elderly belong are ones through which they help the needy. By comparison, slightly *less* than half the groups to which younger adults belong are ones which help the sick or elderly (44 and 41 percent); while just over half of the groups to which younger adults belong help the poor or other needy (52 and 62 percent). Still, it is only in helping other older people in need that these differences are significant.

More differences appear in the amount of time older and younger adults spend volunteering with groups that help those in need. Here, older men and women spend significantly more hours helping the sick (54 versus 29 hours per year), as well as significantly more hours helping other older people (57 versus 28 hours per year), than do younger adults. The elderly also spend more time helping all types of needy combined than do younger adults (84 versus 50 hours per year). Age, however, does not significantly affect the proportion of volunteer time that is spent helping the needy. Approximately one third of the time both older and younger adults spend volunteering is devoted to helping those in need. Overall, then, while older men and women may spend more hours helping the needy, the proportion of their volunteer hours that is devoted to charity work does not significantly differ from that their younger counterparts spend.

Age, Gender, Marriage and Giving Care

The effects of age on giving care appear to vary across dimensions of help, types of recipients, and types of support. The question remains, however, as to the extent to which these patterns are a consequence of age, or of other social characteristics and competing demands for care. To address these questions, we use ordinary least squares regression analysis (OLS), and introduce controls for variables shown to affect helping others in previous research. These are gender, family income, and race. The results of these regressions are presented in Table 3.5.

In general, the effects of age, gender, and marriage are all quite significant across types of recipient and dimensions of care. The direction of these effects differs, however, depending on whether we are considering number of people, or hours of help to family, friends, or others. Age significantly decreases the number of friends and neighbors helped, as well as the amount of time spent helping them. In contrast, age significantly *increases* number of group memberships, as well as the number of hours spent helping kin — suggesting that older men and women continue to be deeply involved in helping kin (even though they may help fewer of them) and have the potential, at least, for helping others through the volunteer groups to which they belong.[1]

Table 3.5
OLS Regression of Number of Persons Helped and Hours of Help on Age, Gender, Marriage, Income, and Race

	# Kin	# Friends	# Groups	Hours Kin	Hours Friends	Hours Volunteering
Age	-.01 (.01)	-.03** (.01)	.03** (.01)	.39* (.19)	-.11* (.06)	.09 (.06)
Gender[a]	-1.29*** (.35)	-1.30*** (.40)	.69* (.31)	-26.34*** (5.76)	-5.21** (1.79)	.31 (1.81)
Marriage[b]	-2.01*** (.54)	.70 (.61)	.25 (.47)	-29.46*** (8.79)	6.32* (2.74)	.85 (2.76)
Income[c]	1.48 (.93)	1.71+ (1.05)	5.39*** (.81)	1.58 (15.12)	8.14+ (4.71)	7.53 (4.74)
Race[d]	.34 (.44)	.73 (.49)	-.58 (.38)	-18.89** (7.13)	2.32 (2.22)	-6.28** (2.24)
Constant	4.89*** (.86)	3.67*** (.98)	-1.20 (.76)	39.69** (14.09)	11.26** (4.39)	6.03 (4.42)
R^2	.13*** (2.76)	.08*** (3.12)	.15*** (2.42)	.10*** (44.96)	.07*** (14.01)	.04* (14.10)

Notes: Unstandardized beta coefficients (β). Standard error in parentheses. Symbols indicate significance levels: $+\leq.10$; $*\leq.05$; $**\leq.01$; $***\leq.001$. N=324. [a] Men=1; Women=0. [b] Widowed=0. Married=1; Married=0. [c] Family income in dollars, x 10,000. [d] White=1; Black=0.

Certainly, the demands of child rearing and employment characteristic of younger and middle adult years decrease the amount of time available for helping kin outside the nuclear household, as well as for belonging to a larger number of volunteer associations. Yet, while competing demands from child rearing and employment may reduce some aspects of giving care, these also integrate men and women into wider networks of friends and neighbors to whom they give more hours of help than do their older counterparts.

Other Factors Affecting Giving Care

While age clearly affects help to both kin and nonkin, it does not operate alone. Both gender and marriage significantly affect the number of people and amount of time spent helping others. In fact, the effects of gender are generally more significant, as well as more consistent, than those of age across types of care. Women, regardless of age, help significantly *more* kin and *more* friends than do men. Women also spend significantly more time helping kin (approximately 26 hours more a month) and friends (approximately 5 hours more a month) than do men. In contrast, men belong to significantly more volunteer associations than do women.[2] Women, then, regardless of age, are significantly more involved in giving help to people they know than are men, while men appear to be somewhat more involved in formal volunteerism (at least in terms of number of group memberships) than are women.

Marriage also significantly affects both the number of people helped and the amount of time spent helping others. As with age, these effects vary across dimensions of care. On the one hand, marriage increases the number of kin helped and the amount of time spent helping them. Those who are married (coded in Table 3.5 as "0") help an average of two more relatives, and spend nearly 30 more hours a month helping relatives, than their widowed counterparts.[3] In contrast, marriage significantly *decreases* time spent helping friends by more than 6 hours a month. Marriage is also associated with belonging to fewer volunteer groups, spending less time volunteering, and helping fewer friends; however, these effects do not reach statistical significance. The degree to which marriage integrates men and women into networks of care, then, varies across types of recipients: marriage expands help to kin, at the same time that it restricts help to nonkin—especially friends and neighbors.

SUMMARY AND DISCUSSION

Giving care is characterized by both continuity and change as people age. Neither disengagement theory nor continuity theory provides an adequate explanation for the breadth and depth of older men's and women's involvement in helping family, friends and others. Neither image of the elderly—as withdrawn or as an untapped source of volunteers—is completely accurate. The answers are "Both" and "It depends."

On the one hand, older men and women tend to spend less time, providing fewer types of help to fewer people they know—especially friends—than do younger adults. The elderly also drop many age-specific volunteer associations, particularly groups oriented toward employment or having young children at home. Both of these findings support the broad outlines of disengagement theory—that aging involves a gradual withdrawal from a broad range of activities and relationships with others.

Yet, the elderly are highly involved in caring for kin—spending more than 34 hours a month providing a wide range of help and support to kin, and more than 26 hours a month to adult children in particular. Clearly, those studies which emphasize the growing dependence of the elderly on their adult children tell only half the story. Whether it is doing the "little things"—giving day-to-day encouragement about work or family, or picking up a packet of Jell-O at the supermarket—or providing substantial help and support in times of crisis, caring for adult children remains an important focus in the lives of older parents.

By themselves, these trends might be interpreted as support for the idea that the elderly disengage out of the community and "into the family" (Smith, 1966). But in this analysis, patterns of help to those who are neither family nor friends—helping strangers through volunteer associations—suggest an alternative interpretation. Rather than disengaging from participation in volunteer groups, a carefully constructed list of group memberships reveals that group membership shifts as men and women age. While the elderly may no longer belong to some of the groups in which younger adults are active, the elderly *do* belong to other types of volunteer associations. Thus, service groups, groups specifically for the elderly or for veterans, replace youth or job oriented groups. Total group membership remains essentially the same.

Not only do the elderly belong to similar numbers of volunteer groups, they actually increase their hours of involvement relative to younger adults. This is particularly true for groups that help different types of needy. If there is to be a new wave of volunteers then, the state may be correct in looking to the old, rather than the young, in its efforts to encourage unpaid help within the community.

This part of the analysis also suggests, however, that efforts to reengage the elderly in giving care may be misplaced. While both disengagement and continuity theories focus on age itself as a determinant of helping behavior, this analysis demonstrates that the elderly do not simply withdraw into helping kin. Nor do they simply continue (or replace) previous helping roles. Indeed, if aging is characterized by disengagement, it might be more accurately described as disengagement from *obligations* to care, rather than disengagement from helping relationships more generally. Two distinct trends suggest why this might be the case. First, in every case of informal help—except that involving the strongest normative obligations to care (e.g., caring for adult children)—older men and women are less involved than are their younger counterparts. Second, in cases involving the *least* obligation to care (helping strangers), the elderly are as engaged—even *more* engaged, in terms of hours—as are younger adults.

A number of respondents were quick to point out that one of the great freedoms of aging is the freedom *not* to feel obligated. In doing so, they echo the sentiments of the woman quoted in the beginning of this chapter — that they are no longer as constrained by obligations to help others, but can say no. As one woman put it, "I've gotten to the stage where I *can* say no. I couldn't before, but now I can. When you're young, you don't know enough or don't have the nerve, but sometimes it's better."

These trends reveal something first about the significance of caring for children: that for many it goes beyond obligation. Sometimes, women recognized and tried to explain the depth of their connectedness. As one woman said as she discussed the help she gives her adult children, "I do it out of love in my heart. I don't do it out of obligation; they're part of us."

At the same time these patterns of help also reveal something about the potential efficacy of policies intended to mobilize the unused talents of the elderly. It is striking that other than helping adult children, the only instance in which the elderly provide more care than the young is that which is, by definition, not obligatory, but voluntary. To the extent, then, that the new volunteerism attempts to "reobligate" the elderly in caring for those who are neither family nor friends, these policies may result in greater resistance within the very population they are intended to mobilize.

Finally, these findings suggest that part of what shapes the help older people give others is not only age, but both gender and marriage.

NOTES

1. One of the reasons age increases hours helping kin is that younger people are less likely than older people to have adult children to help. When hours of help to kin is reestimated for kin *other than* adult children, the effects of age are still positive. Older people spend more time helping kin—whether kin in general, or kin other than adult children—than do their younger counterparts.

2. Men also spend slightly more time volunteering than do women. However, this difference is quite small and is not statistically significant.

3.   Because of sample size and because data were collected in order to compare married and widowed women over 60 in particular, no data are available for either divorced or never married men and women, or for widowed men.

Part II

Gender and Giving Care

A large body of research has established a gender based division of labor both inside and outside the home. In it, women provide the majority of family care—whether to small children, aging parents, in-laws or more distant relatives (Cantor, 1983; DiLeonardo, 1987; Goetting, 1986; Mancini and Blieszner, 1989; Rosenthal, 1985). While several studies have demonstrated that women continue to do most of the work inside the home even after husbands have retired (Altergott and Duncan, 1987; Brubaker and Hennon, 1982; Rexroat and Shehan, 1987; Szinovacz, 1989), very few analyses have examined how gender affects the work older people do in caring for others outside the home. Yet, just as gender differences in domestic work persist after retirement, gender differences in helping those outside the home may also persist into old age. The extent to which they do would lend support to theories of care which argue that gender differences—primarily women's propensity to mother, to nurture, to feel greater connectedness and responsibility toward others—are the result, not of the structure of men's and women's adult lives, but of personality differences rooted in early psychosocial development.

Part II addresses this question by assessing the ways in which gender affects whether, what, and to whom older men and women give unpaid help and support. It focuses on married women and men age 60 and older and examines gender differences in informal help to family and friends, the ways in which characteristics of the recipients shape the help older men and women give, and gender differences in formal help given others through volunteer efforts.

Part II

Gender and Giving Care

4

Gender and Informal Help
to Family and Friends

BACKGROUND

Comparing the patterns of help given by older and younger adults hints at the continuing importance of giving care in the lives of older men and women. Yet, we know relatively little about the breadth and depth of older people's involvement in helping others, or the ways in which these are shaped by gender. Examining gender differences in the size of older people's helping networks, the amount of time spent helping family and friends, and the types of care provided is one means of uncovering something of the depth and variety of older men's and women's giving care. Gender differences in these patterns may reflect a greater ethic of care among women. They may, however, also reflect the power of employment to expand opportunities for helping others for some, while limiting them for others. For men and women currently over 60—a cohort in which men have had a more consistent and continuous history of employment—employment may have a greater effect on what and to whom they provide care than does gender itself.

Helping Adult Children and Grandchildren

Previous research suggests that older men and women may provide different types of care to adult children, as well as grandchildren. Elderly mothers play a significant role as "family watchdogs"—coming to the aid of adult children especially in times of crisis (Troll, 1983); as family historians (Gladstone, 1988), and as support for both child rearing (Aldous, 1987, 1985; Burton and Bengtson, 1985) and housework (Smith, 1966). Grandmothers also act as significant stress buffers in providing housing, child care, and emotional support after divorce (Cherlin and Furstenberg, 1986; Furstenberg et al., 1983; Gladstone, 1988; Hagestad, 1982; M. Johnson, 1988). They are also actively involved in helping adult children cope with the death of a spouse or family member (Bankoff, 1984; Greenberg and Becker, 1988).

In contrast, older fathers mostly provide financial assistance for housing (Kennedy and Stokes, 1982) and advice about finances and careers (Bengtson, 1985; Rossi and Rossi, 1990). Hagestad (1985) summarizes these gender differences in grandparenting roles in terms of traditional definitions of grandmothers as "minister of the interior," and grandfathers as "head of the family."

Helping Other Relatives

Previous research has less to say about the ways in which gender affects the help older people give to kin other than adult children and grandchildren. Nevertheless, a few studies suggest gender may affect both the types and the amount of care older men and women provide to other relatives. Both women and men give emotional support to siblings (Goetting, 1986). Sisters, however, may play a more central role than brothers in providing emotional support to siblings—especially after the death of a spouse (McGhee, 1985; O'Bryant, 1988). At the same time, retirement seems to intensify this type of caring for men—suggesting that employment, along with gender, may affect not only the amount, but also the types of care provided.

Other research suggests older men and women also differ in the amount of help they give kin. Although no studies specifically examine hours of help or number of kin helped, Fischer (1982) finds older women's networks of kin decline less rapidly than do older men's. While network size does not necessarily reflect the amount of care given, it does, at the least, establish plausible boundaries for involvement in helping kin. There may, then, also be significant gender differences in the amount of help older people give to kin.

Helping Friends and Neighbors

As with helping relatives, most previous research on help given to nonkin limits itself to frequency of interaction. Very few analyses focus on the specific types or amount of care older men and women give friends and neighbors. Nevertheless, several studies find significant differences in older men's and women's relations with friends and neighbors—relations which provide the context for exchanges of help and support.

Early research by Rosow (1967) and Townsend (1957) argues that older women have more contact with neighbors than do elderly men. Similarly, elderly women appear to have more confidants (Hoyt et al., 1980) and to be more involved with friends and neighbors than are older men (Altergott, 1985;

Fischer 1982).

Previous research also suggests a number of other factors that, along with gender, affect interaction with (and by implication, caring for) friends and neighbors. Gender differences in patterns of friendship may be exaggerated by class. Booth (1972), for example, finds that middle class men have a greater number of friends than do middle class women, but that these differences disappear within the working class. Retirement also variously affects older men's and women's relations with friends—increasing contact with friends among women, while having little impact on contact with friends among men (Farrell and Rosenberg, 1981; Verburgge, 1983). This negative association between employment and women's helping friends is also suggested by studies finding that both full and part time employment reduce women's interaction with neighbors (Fischer, 1982; O'Donnell; 1985).

HYPOTHESES

Women's greater involvement with family and friends suggests gender differences in giving care may persist into old age. We might expect, then, that older women spend more time and help a greater number of people—whether relatives or friends and neighbors—than do older men.

Gender may also affect the types of care older people provide. On the one hand, gender differences in types of help may be less apparent in old age than they are earlier in life. Older men may be more involved in providing nurturing, more expressive types of support, while older women may be active in giving advice and financial support. On the other hand, as continuity theory would suggest, a lifetime pattern of providing particular kinds of help and support may persist beyond retirement into old age. Thus, women's roles as mothers and kinkeepers and men's roles as fathers and breadwinners may be reflected in gender differences that are greatest for those types of help that are most consistent with women's nurturing and men's economic roles.

Along with gender, findings from previous research suggest a number of social-structural forces may affect helping others in old age. Higher income, in particular, provides resources for greater and more flexible care. Employment also provides greater opportunities for helping others—particularly nonkin—at the same time that it constrains the amount of time available for providing that care. Gender differences in access to resources—whether greater contact with others through employment or higher income—may play as significant a role in shaping patterns of help among the elderly—contradicting the notion that gender differences in help are rooted in a greater ethic of care among women. To the extent that this is the case, we might expect gender to drop out as a significant predictor of giving care, when the effects of income and employment are controlled.[1]

ANALYSIS

The vast majority of older men and women are involved in giving some sort of help to someone they know. Ninety-four percent of older men and 96 percent of older women helped at least one person in the previous month. Over 90 percent of both men and women also helped at least one relative. The majority of both older men and older women also helped at least one friend or neighbor in the previous month (53 and 69 percent; $p \leq .10$).

While most older people are clearly not dependent on the help they receive without providing some degree of help in return, older men and women are not similarly involved in helping others. Older women's networks of care are significantly larger than men's—consistent with the hypothesis that women remain kinkeepers in old age. Older women help a significantly larger *number* of kin (4.91 versus 3.97), and a larger number of people overall (6.86 versus 5.34) than do older men. Among kin, older women help a larger number of kin related by marriage than do older men (.85 versus .50), but not significantly more kin related by blood (4.06 versus 3.47). Although these differences are significant at only the $p \leq .10$ level, they suggest that marriage integrates women into a set of caring relations with in-laws in a way it does not for men. Older women are not only kinkeepers for their own kin, but for their husband's kin as well.

In contrast, older men and women do not significantly differ in the number of friends and neighbors helped (1.95 versus 1.38). Where there is the most obligation to provide care (their own kin), and where there is the least obligation to care (friends and neighbors), the extent of older men's and women's helping others does not differ. Where gender matters—and where older women consistently help more—is in helping kin in general—especially in-laws—and in helping people overall.

These differences may be evidence of women's greater sense of connectedness to others. They may also, however, obscure social-structural variables affecting older men's and women's abilities and opportunities to provide care. Continuity of help giving roles and the power of employment to expand networks of nonkin may help to explain a lack of gender difference in the number of own kin and friends helped. At the same time, resources such as higher income or better health may help to explain gender differences—or lack of differences—in the help older men and women provide. Holding constant the effects of age and race, regression analysis allows an examination of gender in conjunction with resources and demands that may affect giving care. These are family income, health, history of helping others, and current employment status (employed or unemployed—either retired or homemakers).[2] The results of this analysis are given in Table 4.1.

Table 4.1
OLS Regression of Number of Persons Helped on Gender, Age, Health, Income, Race, Employment and History of Helping Others

	# Persons	# Kin	# Own Kin	# In-Laws	# Friends
Gender[a]	-1.60 (1.02)	-1.07 (.75)	-.57 (.62)	-.51 (.32)	-.53 (.52)
Age	-.10 (.09)	-.06 (.06)	-.05 (.05)	-.00 (.03)	-.05 (.05)
Health	-.82 (.58)	-.44 (.43)	-.41 (.36)	-.03 (.18)	-.37 (.30)
Income[b]	2.87 (2.72)	1.17 (2.00)	.41 (1.67)	.75 (.84)	1.70 (1.38)
History of Help[c]	.34 (.16)*	.24 (.12)*	.15 (.10)	.10 (.05)+	.09 (.08)
Race[d]	1.53 (1.17)	1.07 (.86)	.76 (.72)	.32 (.36)	.46 (.60)
Employment[e]	.32 (1.09)	.87 (.80)	.88 (.67)	-.02 (.34)	-.54 (.56)
Constant	8.76 (6.21)	5.27 (4.57)	4.98 (3.81)	.39 (1.93)	3.41 (3.61)
R^2	.32 (3.93)***	.24 (2.89)**	.24 (2.41)*	.21 (1.22)*	.23 (2.00)*

Notes: Unstandardized beta coefficients (ß). Standard error in parentheses. Symbols indicate significance levels: $+\leq.10$; $*\leq.05$; $**\leq.01$; $***\leq.001$. Men, N=32; Women, N=55. [a] Men=1; Women=0. [b] History of help=number of family, friends and others to whom respondents gave significant help with finances, housing or sick care in the past. [c] Family income in dollars, x 10,000. [d] White=1; Black=0. [e] Employed: Yes=1, No (retired or homemaker)=0.

When the effects of resources are examined along with those of gender, gender drops out as a significant predictor of breadth of care—regardless of the type of recipient being helped. Instead, what most consistently affects number of persons helped is previous history of helping others. Older men and women who have been more heavily involved in helping family and friends in the past are currently involved in helping more people overall, as well as more kin and more in-laws than are those with less history of giving care. The effects of other explanatory variables are all in the expected directions. However, none of these other social characteristics has any significant effect on the number of people older men and women help.

Hours of Care

If gender differences in the number of people helped tell us something about the breadth of help older men and women give, we see the depth of their involvement in the amount of time they devote to helping others. Older women spend more than twice as much time helping people overall per month as do older men (59 versus 23 hours; $p \leq .001$). Older women also spend approximately twice as much time helping kin (52 versus 21 hours; $p \leq .01$), and almost three times as much time helping friends (6.89 versus 2.38 hours; $p \leq .01$) as do older men. While the sizes of older men's and older women's helping networks may be similar, women clearly spend more time helping others, regardless of the type of recipient being helped.

These differences may be a result of the competing demands of employment for time that might be spent helping others, or of poorer health among older men, or of income that could purchase greater "free" time for helping. Using regression analysis, it is possible to examine the degree to which social-structural variables (such as employment) and social characteristics (such as age and health) help to explain gender differences in the amount of time spent helping others (Table 4.2).

Even with controls, older women provide over 28 more hours a month helping people they know than do older men. Older women also spend about 5 ½ hours more a month helping friends than do older men. Thus, while the breadth of help older men and women give to family and friends may be similar (both help similar numbers of kin and friends), the depth of older women's help is clearly greater than men's—even controlling for the competing demands of employment.

In fact, other than gender, the only other social characteristics that affect hours of help are age and employment. Somewhat surprisingly, being older is associated with slightly more time helping friends, as is employment. Although employment does not affect the *number* of friends helped, it significantly

Table 4.2
OLS Regression of Hours of Help on Gender, Age, Health, Income, Race, Employment, and History of Helping Others

	Total Hours	Hours Kin	Hours Friends
Gender	-28.18+ (15.62)	-22.93 (15.41)	-5.52* (2.34)
Age	.74 (1.35)	.43 (1.34)	.34+ (.20)
Health	-10.52 (8.98)	-9.57 (8.86)	-.77 (1.35)
Income	6.76 (41.74)	1.27 (41.19)	8.90 (6.26)
History of Help	2.81 (2.52)	2.57 (2.48)	.21 (.38)
Race	-14.66 (18.05)	-16.40 (17.82)	1.36 (2.71)
Employment	-3.74 (16.77)	-8.28 (16.55)	4.35+ (2.52)
Constant	-12.40 (95.43)	4.86 (94.19)	-20.11 (14.31)
R^2	.20+ (60.40)	.17 (59.62)	.22* (9.06)

Notes: Unstandardized beta coefficients (ß). Symbols indicate significance levels: $+\leq.10$; $*\leq.05$; $**\leq.01$; $***\leq.001$. Controlling for having living parents, parents-in-law, and adult children. Standard errors in parentheses. Men, N=32; Women, N=55. See Table 4.1 for a description of independent variables.

increases the hours older men and women spend helping friends and neighbors. It may be, then, that older men and women who remain employed spend more time helping fewer people, than those who are retired or unemployed.

Perhaps more importantly, employment has roughly the same effect on hours of care to friends as does gender. Employed elderly spend approximately 4 hours more a month helping friends than do their nonemployed counterparts—

suggesting that the opportunities to help friends made available through employment are as significant in shaping the amount of time older men and women spend helping friends as is gender itself.

Helping kin is a different matter. When the effects of other explanatory variables are controlled, gender drops out as a predictor of hours helping kin. Although older women spend 23 hours more a month helping relatives than do men, this difference is not significant.[3] Somewhat surprisingly, none of these other variables shows a significant effect on hours of help to kin or on hours of help overall. Regardless of resources or the competing demands of employment, older men spend essentially the same amount of time helping relatives as do older women. Helping kin, then, appears to be much less dependent on personal resources—and on gender—than is helping friends and neighbors.

Caring for Family and Friends: Personal Explanations

Part of what we may be seeing here may reflect two different sets of motivations for providing care. On the one hand there is the obligation to help relatives—one that clearly takes precedence over caring for friends and neighbors (as reflected both in greater numbers of kin helped and in more hours helping kin), and one that appears to be rather insensitive to personal resources such as income and health. On the other hand, there are affective motivators—feelings of concern and affection that may play a significant role, in particular, in helping friends. The preceding quantitative analysis hints at the importance of these in shaping patterns of help among older men and women. While we have no data on the strength of kinship obligations, the importance of both obligation and affection in motivating giving care is supported by the words of the respondents themselves. As one retired woman explained, "Helping family is a necessity. They would expect it. Family you are stuck with. Good, bad, indifferent. You are stuck with your family. I feel obligated to help them." In contrast, this same woman explained motivations for helping friends in terms of affection and reciprocity:

> You've chosen your friends. They are your friends because there is something between you, they're people that you admire for one reason or another, something makes you click. When friends need help, you just do it. They do for you, you do for them. You don't think about things like that because you just love one another, right?

At the same time, while not always as clearly, older men expressed similar sentiments. As one 67 year-old man explained when asked whether helping friends was any different from helping relatives, "If I had to make a choice, I'd choose helping the family. If we had to be in two places at the same time, we'd give a chance to the family first." Although not specifically discussing obligations to kin, there are in this man's comments elements of the same hierarchy of caring expressed by older women: that obligations to help family clearly take priority over obligations to help friends and neighbors.

Older men also expressed motivations similar to those of older women for helping friends and neighbors. While less likely to describe helping friends out of "love," older men did talk about the importance of shared interests and norms of reciprocity in helping friends and neighbors. As one professional man explained:

> Well, I think the friends that I help are people that probably share some of the same interests that I have. So that the advice and help or whatever that I give them is just sharing my experience with them. I think friends can be just as close as relatives—that's why they're friends. The only thing is, if there is someone that doesn't have time for me, well that's fine and dandy too. Because maybe what I will do is devote a little bit more of the time that I have to the people that have time for me. You respond to people in the same manner that they respond to you. If someone gives you 50 percent, then you ought to give them at least 50 percent back.

These sentiments were echoed by a number of working class men as well—many of whom spoke at length about their history of helping others and the importance of reciprocity in helping friends and neighbors. Some of these had come from rural backgrounds, and this was reflected in the kinds of help and support given to friends:

> I used to fix my neighbor's machinery and he'd plow my land. He was a potato farmer, and I'd fix his lights or motors. You wouldn't look for pay 'cause one friend would help you in return. If anyone needs help, you're there to help. And if we need help, the neighbors would come and help us.

These men's and women's comments suggest two things. First, respondents clearly articulated the same hierarchy of care evident in the quantitative analysis—that helping kin takes precedence over helping friends and neighbors. Although affection plays a role—often a major role—in helping family, with or without affection, obligation is often an effective motivator for helping kin. Second, respondents—particularly middle class women—tended to emphasize affection as an important motivation in helping friends. Yet the strength of obligation as a motivation for giving help is evident for helping friends as well—tacitly making its appearance as reciprocity.[4] Thus, while norms of reciprocity tended to be more apparent in older men's explanations for helping friends, reciprocity motivated older women's helping friends and neighbors as well. Still, for older women, the emphasis tended to be on affection, rather than obligation—friends being "freely" chosen, and help "freely" given—at least without the same degree of felt obligation to help as with kin.

Types of Care

Gender also affects the types of care provided. Older women do almost twice as many practical tasks for family and friends as do older men (7.85 versus 3.91 tasks per month; $p \leq .01$).[5] They also give twice as much personal help as do older men (4.24 versus 2.19 personal tasks per month; $p \leq .01$).[6] However, older men and women do not significantly differ in giving material support—whether money, gifts or goods (approximately 4 versus 3 tasks per month).

Rather than a decline in gender differences in types of support as men and women age, these data suggest the alternative hypothesis—that gender differences in the particular types of care persist in old age. The same lack of a division of labor found among younger and middle aged men and women (Gerstel and Gallagher, 1990a) is found in older men's and women's informal help as well. Older women do significantly more of a broad range of tasks, mostly clustered in domestic and nurturing activities—while older men do not provide significantly more of *any* kind of support—whether practical, personal, or material—than do older women.

Even when controls are introduced for other possible explanatory variables such as health, family income, employment and age, gender remains a significant predictor of each category of help and support (Table 4.3). Older women provide significantly more practical help (especially laundry, meals, repairs, sick care, child care and cleaning) and more personal help (especially talk about personal problems and concerns) than do men.

While gender clearly affects the kinds of help older men and women give others, it does not act alone. The resources on which older people may draw also have a significant effect on the types of help provided. Not surprisingly, higher income increases material help—particularly gifts of money. More importantly, women with similar financial resources actually provide *more* material help than do men. Thus, differential access to resources that enable giving care—in this case, income—plays an important role in shaping the types of help older men and women provide.

Gender differences in the types of care provided may also be shaped by older men's and women's access to the time required to provide that care. Competing demands from employment, for example, may limit time consuming tasks, affecting the amount of practical help older men in particular may be able

Table 4.3
OLS Regression of Types of Help on Gender, Age, Health, Income, History of Help, Race, and Employment

	Practical Help	Personal Help	Material Help
Gender	-5.80 (1.67)***	-2.83 (.81)***	-2.09 (1.03)*
Age	-.15 (.14)	-.04 (.07)	-.05 (.09)
Health	.46 (.96)	-.22 (.46)	.02 (.59)
Income	-.55 (4.46)	3.31 (2.15)	6.80 (2.75)*
History of Help	.48 (.27)+	.09 (.13)	.24 (.17)
Race	2.90 (1.93)	.11 (.93)	1.69 (1.19)
Employment	3.71 (1.79)*	1.18 (.87)	1.05 (1.11)
Constant	8.16 (10.19)	3.60 (4.93)	1.62 (6.27)
R^2	.35 (6.45)***	.34 (3.12)***	.37 (3.98)***

Notes: Unstandardized beta coefficients (ß). Symbols indicate significance levels: +≤.10; *≤.05; **≤.01; ***≤.001. Controlling for having living parents, parents-in-law, and adult children. Standard errors in parentheses. Men, N=32; Women, N=55. See Table 4.1 for a description of independent variables.

to provide. However, employment appears to have the opposite effect than what might be expected   increasing, rather than decreasing, the amount of practical help given to family and friends. The main effect of employment is not to limit time available for helping others, rather employment appears to expand the pool of potential recipients and thus increase the total amount of practical help provided.

SUMMARY AND DISCUSSION

Overall, women's involvement in giving care extends into old age. Older women spend significantly more time helping a greater number of people overall and a greater number of kin, than do older men. Older women are also more likely to help friends and spend significantly more time doing so than do older men.   Even at the level of individual tasks, older women consistently do more—especially in providing the practical and personal kinds of help that are extensions of their domestic and nurturing roles. Older men's giving care only matches that of older women in the number of own kin and the number of friends helped. This suggests the strength of obligations in motivating care to one's own kin, as well as the importance of employment in expanding opportunities for helping nonkin. While older men may help as many friends and as many blood relatives as do older women, older women are overwhelmingly more involved in almost every other dimension of care. Older women not only are kinkeepers: they are "friend keepers" as well.

At the same time, gender does not operate alone in shaping patterns of help among the elderly. The resources on which older men and women draw in helping others have a significant impact on the help they provide. More importantly, these resources help to explain some of the differences between older men and women in the amount of time and types of care they give family and friends.

This is most clearly seen in the hours of care to kin and in the number of material tasks older men and women perform overall. On the one hand, when personal resources such as health, income and employment are controlled for, older women do not spend more time caring for kin than do older men. Although none of these variables is individually significant, together they cause gender to drop out as a predictor of hours of care to kin. This suggests that the help older men give kin may be limited by their greater rates of employment or declining health. Perhaps more importantly, while gender initially appears to make no difference in the amount of material help older men and women provide, this lack of difference disappears when one controls for income. Gender differences in access to the resources that make helping others possible may help to explain gendered patterns of help among the elderly.

Finally, it is important to note that gender seems to matter least where helping is most obligatory—to one's own kin. Although older women help significantly more in-laws and more kin overall than do older men, older men help as many of their own kin as do older women. In these ways, gender differences in actual help parallel gender differences in felt obligation to different types of kin. Thus, just as men and women feel similarly obligated to help their most proximate kin (Rossi and Rossi, 1990), this study finds older men and women are similarly involved in doing so. And, as women generally feel more obligated to help less proximate kin than do men (in-laws, for example), similarly, the women in this study differed from men the most—doing more—in terms of helping those on the periphery of felt obligation.

These patterns of help also point to the importance of marriage in structuring what and to whom older men and women give help and support. Marriage clearly provides an expanded network of kin to both men and women. However, the effect of marriage on giving care is to increase the number of people and amount of time older women—not men—spend helping others. While older men may help as many of their own kin as do older women, the greater burden of caring for kin in general, and in-laws in particular, is assumed by older women. Marriage, then, plays a central role in integrating women into a larger network of kin to whom they provide care.

NOTES

1. Most wives in this sample were not employed, or had very low personal incomes. In order to prevent representing women as disproportionately poor relative to men, total family income is used as an indicator of the material resources on which older men and women might draw in helping others.

2. If this analysis is repeated with an additional variable controlling for work history (whether respondents had ever worked for pay in the past), the results are essentially the same. Work history has no significant effect on either the number of family or the number of friends helped.

3. The same is true for hours helping adult children (data not shown). While older women spend approximately 15 hours a month more than older men helping adult children, this difference is not significant when the effects of other explanatory variables are controlled.

4. This was particularly true within the middle class. Perhaps where the economic nature of caring for friends is less clearly perceived, the ideology of friendship based on affection and love distracts from the obligations implied by the notion of reciprocity. The economic nature of caring and the importance of the obligation to reciprocate help to friends are seen more clearly in the working class. More than one respondent echoed the words of the women in Carol Stack's All Our Kin (1974), saying "What goes around, comes around," even at great economic cost to themselves. One woman, about to be evicted, explained her difficulty in saving money to pay for a truck to help her move:

> I used to have a car, but I finally got rid of it. I used to give rides to friends all the time. I couldn't even start it up without someone asking me for a ride. Now I have a problem. I'm moving to a smaller apartment and have to get rid of some of this stuff and move the rest, so I'm trying to raise money to move. Sometimes it makes me a little short when I loan friends money and then don't get it back when they say. We exchange money practically every day if we've got any. I've been trying to collect what people owe me. I need it now and none of them have it, or that's what they say. It's near Christmas and everyone's cryin' the blues.

The key here is that this woman was disturbed, not that her friends and neighbors didn't love her, but that they were not reciprocating the economic help she had given them in the past.

5. In particular, older women give more help with practical tasks that are an extension of their domestic roles, such as doing laundry (.96 versus .22; $p \leq .001$), preparing a meal (2.6 versus 1; $p \leq .001$), helping someone who is sick (.81 versus .34; $p \leq .05$), and cleaning or household chores (.53 versus .13; $p \leq .05$). Although older men give as much of some types of practical help as older women—giving rides, doing yard work, watching a home while someone is away, visiting in the hospital, or giving help with banking—there is no practical task for which older men give significantly more than do older women.

6. This is especially so for personal help in the form of talk about personal problems and concerns (3.67 versus 1.63; $p \leq .001$), but not more advice about employment (.26 versus .13) or other matters (.44 versus .40).

5

Gender and the Recipients of Care

INTRODUCTION

Helping others may be motivated by a wide range of factors. The need of the recipient, the ability of the giver, and the relationship between the two combine in one individual's decision to help another. Motivations may be related to the characteristics of the recipient, as well as the context in which care is given. These characteristics and the ways in which they affect giving care differently for older men and women are the focus of this chapter. By linking the help older people give to the characteristics of those they help, we can assess the degree to which older men and women may exhibit differences in their responses to the needs of others: differences that speak to the existence—and persistence—of a peculiar ethic of care among women.

BACKGROUND

Previous research contains only hints of the ways in which the help older men and women give are affected by the characteristics of those they help. The gender, marital status, and geographic proximity of the recipient are among the most frequently mentioned.

The gender of the recipient affects helping others in two ways. First, older men and women may be inclined to help those who are similarly male or female. To the extent that homogeneity of gender influences giving care, older women ought to focus on helping other women, while older men ought to focus on helping other men. Gender may also, however, be understood as a rough indicator of the relative need of the recipient. Older women, for example, may help other women not only because they are inclined to help others who are like them, but because they understand women earn less when they are employed and have primary responsibility for both domestic work and child care regardless of whether or not they work outside the home (Berk, 1988; Coverman, 1989;

Hochschild, 1989; Thompson and Walker, 1989).

Women do report feeling greater obligation to help others, in general, than do men—especially greater obligation to other women, and to unmarried women in particular (Rossi and Rossi, 1990). Older women also interact more with women than do older men, although both older men and women interact more with women than with men (Booth, 1972; Hill et al., 1970). If helping others is motivated by obligation and mirrors interaction, then we ought to find similar patterns of gender difference in the help older men and women give family and friends. Both may be inclined to help women more than men, but this inclination ought to be greater among older women.

But care is not given only in response to need. Opportunity, ability, and affection must be balanced with the weight of obligation in men's and women's decisions to help another. Geographic proximity, for example, may significantly affect not only to whom but also what types of help are given. Feelings of affection or affinity are of increasing importance when norms of obligations to care are less clear. These characteristics, proximity and affection, facilitate giving care by making it easier, as well as possibly more rewarding, for the giver. Homogeneity of gender also facilitates giving care, to the extent that it reflects women's affinity for helping other women, rather than a response to greater need.

Gender and the Characteristics of Adult Children

Recent research on parent-child that relations suggests normative obligations to provide care are relatively unaffected by the characteristics of adult children (Rossi and Rossi, 1990). Actual patterns of help show that children's characteristics that facilitate giving care   whether geographic proximity or affective closeness   similarly affect help given by both older mothers and older fathers (Rossi and Rossi, 1990; Troll, Miller and Atchley, 1979). Parents give more help to children who live closer and to whom they feel more close than to children who live farther away or to whom they feel less close.

Adult children's gender and marital status have a more complicated set of effects on the help older mothers and fathers provide. Older mothers and fathers both give more help to daughters who are unmarried than to daughters who are married. However, whether sons are married or not has no significant effect on the help either older mothers or older fathers give. It may be that older mothers and fathers are equally sensitive to the needs that may accompany singleness for daughters, more than they are for sons. However, when income is examined along with gender, it appears that both homogeneity of gender and financial need affect the help older parents give adult children. Older women help both daughters and sons with low income. Older men, however, give more help to poorer sons, but not daughters (Rossi and Rossi, 1990).

Together, these findings suggest the help older women give adult children may be slightly more responsive to adult children's needs—particularly those of daughters—than is older men's. This provides some, although limited, support for theories of care that argue for a greater ethic of care among women.

Gender and the Characteristics of Friends

Scattered research also suggests the help older women give friends may be more responsive to the characteristics of those they help than is older men's. Most of this evidence is indirect—coming from studies of interaction and obligation, rather than observations of giving care itself. More specifically, previous research suggests the help older women give friends may be more affected by closeness—whether geographic or affective—than is help from older men. Geographic proximity increases older women's interaction with friends more than that of older men (Rosow, 1967). For men, particularly within this generation, geographic proximity may be less relevant in predicting care to nonkin because men's employment provides opportunities for helping nonkin that are not available to nonemployed women. Older women's friendships are also characterized more by affective closeness than are the friendships of older men (Booth, 1972). To the extent that patterns of help follow these patterns of interaction, care given to friends may be similarly linked to women's feelings of affection for and proximity to friends.

HYPOTHESES

Findings from research on obligations and interaction suggest that geographic proximity, gender, and marriage may also affect the help older men and women give family and friends. Because it is important to separate the influence of gender from that of need, the analysis in this chapter controls for (and examines) the effects of a number of characteristics of the recipients of care. Health and income are included as fairly straightforward indicators of relative need. Affective closeness is included in order to capture something of the quality of the relationship—the context in which care is given.

To the extent that there is a distinctive ethic of care among women, we would expect the help older women provide to be more closely linked to the needs of those they help than is older men's. On the other hand, to the extent that women's predominance in giving care reflects the different structural position of men and women, we would expect to find that the characteristics of the recipients have similar effects on the help older men and women provide.

This chapter focuses specifically on help given to adult children and to friends. This is for two reasons. First, it allows some comparison of the ways in which the characteristics of those helped differ across types of recipients. Adult children and friends are at opposite ends of the spectrum in terms of normative obligations to give care. The characteristics of adult children may have a different set of effects on help given than do the characteristics of friends. Second, data are available for complete sets for these two groups of recipients. To collect information on the characteristics of all kin, regardless of whether or not they were helped, would have taxed the men and women in this study beyond what was reasonable. We do not know, for all types of kin, whether, or in what ways, those helped significantly differed from those not helped. For adult children, this is not an issue. Data were collected on relevant characteristics for all adult children regardless of whether or not they received any help. For friends, we have information on relevant characteristics for all friends helped in the previous month, as well as all friends from whom help was received. There is, of course, the possibility that older men and women have friends to whom they did not give and from whom they did not receive help in the previous month. But this number is probably relatively small—especially since the interviews covered types of help that are not dependent on geographic proximity or physical mobility. Friends, then, are defined in this analysis as those to whom help was given or from whom it was received in the month prior to the interview.

ANALYSIS

First, we compare the amount of help given across types of recipients, using data on the individual types of help given.[1] Then, in order to separate the effects of homogeneity from those of need, we turn to regression analysis, and compare the effects of gender, marriage, and income on the help given.[2]

Caring for Adult Children

The likelihood of providing different types of help and the number of tasks older men and women do for adult daughters and sons are shown in Table 5.1. Looking first at men, we find that older men are just as likely to provide all types of help and support—whether practical, personal or material—to daughters as to sons. In contrast, older women are significantly more likely to give practical and material support to daughters than they are to provide either practical or material help to sons. The gender of an adult child, then, appears to be linked to the likelihood of receiving practical and material help from mothers more than fathers.

This is not the case for the number of tasks, or amount of help, older men and women provide. Older women give slightly more of each type of help to

Table 5.1
Tasks Older Men and Women Perform for Adult Children
(t-Tests)

	Men		Women	
Type of Help[a]	Sons	Daughters	Sons	Daughters
I. Practical Help				
Percent Who Give	.58 (.50)	.52 (.51)	.58 (.50)	.71 (.46)+
Number Tasks	1.42 (1.77)	1.40 (2.08)	2.18 (2.43)	2.88 (2.94)
II. Personal Help				
Percent Who Give	.58 (.50)	.52 (.51)	.63 (.49)	.71 (.46)
Number Tasks	1.00 (1.21)	.76 (.88)	1.24 (1.30)	1.39 (1.41)
III. Material Help				
Percent Who Give	.50 (.51)	.44 (.51)	.45 (.50)	.61 (.49)*
Number Tasks	.88 (.99)	.88 (1.13)	.92 (1.24)	1.29 (1.57)

Notes: Symbols indicate level of significance for a one-tailed test of difference between paired means for daughters and sons, using a separate estimate of variance: +$\leq$.10; *$\leq$.05; **$\leq$.01; ***$\leq$.001. Men, N=32; Women, N=55. Standard deviations are in parentheses. [a] All figures are per month.

daughters than to sons. While older men are as likely to help sons as they are to help daughters, they give slightly more practical and personal support to sons than to daughters. While these trends may suggest homogeneity of gender is an important factor affecting the distribution of help from older parents to adult children, neither of these differences is statistically significant. Both older men and older women give essentially the same number of practical, personal and material tasks to sons as to daughters. These findings are similar to those on parental obligations to help adult children; overall, the gender of an adult child matters very little in determining the help either mothers or fathers provide.

What about other characteristics? How do factors affecting adult children's relative need or likelihood of being helped influence the help older men and women give? Table 5.2 shows the results of regression analysis of types of help on characteristics of the recipients, and select characteristics of those giving care.

Looking first at the effects of income on the types of help older men and women provide, we find children's income has few significant effects on the help older men and women provide. Yet, where income is significant, its effects are quite different for older women and men. Older women give more personal support to both daughters and sons who are poorer than to their wealthier counterparts. In contrast, children's income significantly affects the number of material tasks fathers give sons (but not daughters). Older men give more material help to sons who are poor than to sons who are less poor. Income also significantly affects the number of practical tasks fathers do for sons (but again, not daughters), but in the opposite direction. Older men give more practical support to sons who are wealthier rather than poorer. Both of these effects for men, however, are only marginally significant, at the $p \leq .10$ level.

Two points are important here. First, daughters' income has no effect on any type of help given by fathers. Income for both daughters and sons, however, significantly affects the help older mothers provide. Yet, what older women give adult children with lower income is not more money, but more comfort and advice; while older men give low income sons money, but not advice. Linking older women's personal help to the financial status of their adult children provides limited support, at best, for theories arguing that women are particularly responsive to the needs of others. It highlights, instead, the importance of gender differences in access to resources—particularly material resources—on which older men and women draw in helping others, an issue to which we return in Chapter 8.

As with income, whether or not children are married has different effects on the help they receive from older mothers and fathers. Although each type of help is negatively correlated with children's marriage, children's marriage only affects personal support when children's other characteristics are controlled for. Older fathers give more personal help to sons (but not daughters) who are unmarried. In contrast, older mothers give more personal help to daughters, but not sons. In addition, the direction of this effect for personal care to daughters is positive rather than negative. That is, older mothers give more personal support to daughters who are married than to daughters who are unmarried— perhaps in response to the demands placed on married daughters by their husbands and, in most cases, their own children.[3]

In terms of relative need, Table 5.2 also shows the effects of children's health on the practical, personal and material help older mothers and fathers provide. Although health is not significantly correlated with any of these types of support, from either older men or older women, children's health does affect parental help, net of other children's characteristics. And health, as with other indicators of relative need, differently affects help given by older mothers and fathers, across types of support.

Table 5.2
OLS Regression of Types of Help from Older Men and Women to Adult Children on Respondent and Recipient Characteristics

A. Older Men	Practical Help		Personal Help		Material Help	
	Daughter	Son	Daughter	Son	Daughter	Son
Respondent Characteristics						
Employed[a]	-.17 (.35)	.15 (.27)	.04 (.21)	-.22 (.22)	-.24 (.25)	.15 (.22)
Health	.05 (.20)	-.35 (.21)+	-.01 (.12)	-.03 (.16)	.03 (.14)	-.09 (.16)
Income[b]	1.33 (.83)	-.45 (.89)	1.23 (.51)*	1.05 (.73)	1.80 (.59)**	.93 (.72)
Recipient Characteristics						
Geographic Proximity[c]	-.38 (.08)***	-.36 (.07)***	-.01 (.05)	.01 (.06)	-.11 (.06)*	.01 (.06)
Health[c]	.44 (.23)+	.05 (.18)	.27 (.14)+	.35 (.15)*	.17 (.16)	.25(.15)+
Income[d]	.17 (.28)	.30 (.18)+	.17 (.17)	.06 (.15)	.12 (.20)	-.29 (.15)+
Closeness[d]	.39 (.19)*	.41 (.18)*	.22 (.12)+	.44 (.14)**	.26 (.13)+	.12 (.14)
Marriage[e]	-.29 (.27)	-.27 (.25)	-.13 (.17)	-.40 (.20)*	-.24 (.19)	.13 (.20)
R^2	.49 (.85)***	.49 (.74)***	.25 (.52)	.29 (.61)*	.38 (.61)**	.23 (.60)

Notes: Unstandardized beta coefficients (ß). Significance levels: $+\leq.10$; $*\leq.05$; $**\leq.01$; $***\leq.001$. Standard errors in parentheses. Older men have daughters, N=55; sons, N=54. [a] Employed: yes=1; no=0. [b] Dollars x 10,000. [c] Low score= more proximate residence or better health. [d] Low score=lower income or less emotional closeness. [e] Yes=1; no=0.

Table 5.2
(Continued)

B. Older Women	Practical Help		Personal Help		Material Help	
	Daughters	Sons	Daughters	Sons	Daughters	Sons
Respondent Characteristics						
Employment[a]	-.38 (.34)	-.26 (.38)	.33 (.13)*	-.11 (.16)	-.01 (.19)	.17 (.18)
Health	-.42 (.23)+	-.41 (.21)+	-.13 (.09)	-.18 (.09)*	-.05 (.13)	-.13 (.10)
Income[b]	-.01 (1.01)	-.19 (1.23)	.73 (.40)+	.16 (.49)	2.39 (.56)***	.75 (.56)
Recipient Characteristics						
Geographic Proximity[c]	-.52 (.08)***	-.25 (.10)*	-.06 (.03)+	.01 (.04)	-.14 (.05)**	-.02 (.05)
Health[c]	.16 (.24)	.11 (.25)	.04 (.10)	.09 (.11)	.31 (.14)*	.19 (.12)
Income[d]	-.17 (.24)	-.08 (.27)	-.25 (.10)**	-.25 (.12)*	-.19 (.14)	.07 (.14)
Closeness[d]	.20 (.26)	.28 (.28)	-.01 (.10)	.22 (.12)+	.05 (.14)	.17 (.14)
Marriage[e]	.04 (.35)	-.23 (.43)	.26 (.14)+	-.15 (.19)	.20 (.19)	-.08 (.21)
R²	.41 (1.29)***	.25 (1.31)*	.29 (.51)**	.24 (.57)	.34 (.72)***	.21 (.64)+

Notes: Unstandardized beta coefficients (β). Significance levels: +≤.10; *≤.05; **≤.01; ***≤.001. Standard errors in parentheses. Older women have daughters, N=88; sons, N=74. [a] Employed: yes=1; no=0. [b] Dollars x 10,000. [c] Low score= more proximate residence or better health. [d] Low score=lower income or less emotional closeness. [e] Married: Yes=1; no=0.

Looking first at older men: men give significantly more practical help and more personal help to daughters when daughters are in poorer health. Fathers also give more personal help, as well as more material help, to sons when sons are in poorer health. In contrast, health only significantly affects the amount of material help mothers give adult daughters. Older women give more material help to daughters who are in poorer health than to those who are in better health. To the extent that physical health represents a greater need for care, it would seem that older men are more responsive to this particular type of need among their adult children than are older women.

Finally, Table 5.2 also shows that characteristics that make helping others easier (or possible) have important effects on what and to whom older men and women give care. Adult children's geographic proximity similarly affects help given by both mothers and fathers.[4] Not surprisingly, proximity is most significant in determining the amount of practical support adult daughters and sons receive. Children who live closer receive significantly more practical support from their parents than children who live farther away. Daughters who live closer also receive more material support from both parents, as well as slightly more personal support from their mothers, than do daughters who live farther away.

While the effects of geographic proximity are fairly consistent across types of support and gender of adult child, this is not the case for emotional closeness. Older men give significantly more practical as well as more personal help to both daughters and sons to whom they feel more close than to daughters and sons to whom they feel less close. Older men also give more material help to daughters to whom they feel greater affective closeness. Stated differently, only material help from fathers to sons is unaffected by affective closeness.

Emotional closeness has less effect on the help older women give adult children. Only practical and personal support to daughters is significantly affected by affective closeness. Older mothers give more practical and more personal help to daughters to whom they feel close than to daughters to whom they feel less close. None of the types of help mothers give sons is affected by emotional closeness.

Finally, homogeneity of gender appears to influence the help older women give adult children more than the help given by older men. The characteristics of adult children in cross-gender parent-child dyads are generally no more significant than are the characteristics of adult children in same-gender parent-child dyads in affecting the types of help older fathers provide. For older women, however, the characteristics of adult children are more often significant for same-gender parent-child dyads than for cross-gender dyads. In other words, the types of help older women give are generally more affected by the characteristics of adult daughters than by the characteristics of adult sons, while the types of help older men give are as frequently affected by the characteristics of their adult daughters as by the characteristics of their adult sons.

Together, these findings do not support the hypothesis that the help older women give adult children is any more linked to their children's needs than is help given by older men. Rather, children's characteristics have different effects depending on the type of need, as well as the type of support. Although help from mothers may appear to be more linked to a child's financial need, this is only for personal help and support. Older men's help, in contrast, is more consistently responsive to children's poorer health, across types of support and gender of adult child. The degree to which adult children may be in need significantly affects the help both older women and older men provide   suggesting that the help older women give adult children is no more motivated by an ethic of care than is older men's.

Caring for Friends

Looking at the help older men and women give friends (Table 5.3), we find no significant differences between older men and women in either the number of practical tasks (0.78 versus 1.18) or the number of material tasks (0.53 versus 0.78) done for friends. Older women do, however, give more personal help to friends than do older men. In fact, older women give nearly three times as much personal support to friends as do older men (0.96 versus 0.38).

How do friends' characteristics affect this help? To what extent and in what ways do the characteristics of friends differently affect the help older men and older women provide? Table 5.4 shows the results of regression analyses for

Table 5.3
Number of Tasks Older Men and Women Do for Friends
(t-Tests)

Type of Help[a]	Men[b] (mean #)	Women (mean #)
Practical Help	.78 (1.86)	1.18 (1.91)
Personal Help	.38 (.94)	.96 (1.69)*
Material Help	.53 (1.05)	.78 (1.50)

Notes: Symbols indicate level of significance for a one-tailed test, using a separate estimate of variance: $+\leq.10$; $*\leq.05$; $**\leq.01$; $***\leq.001$. Standard deviations are in parentheses. [a] Mean number of practical, personal and material tasks done for friends and neighbors during the previous month.
[b] Men, N=32; Women, N=55.

Table 5.4
OLS Regression of the Types of Help Older Men and Women Give Friends on Respondent and Recipient Characteristics

	Practical Help		Personal Help		Material Help	
Respondent Characteristics	Men	Women	Men	Women	Men	Women
Employment	-.22 (.26)	-.14 (.21)	.13 (.20)	.01 (.13)	.03 (.20)	.28** (.10)
Health	-.07 (.22)	.15 (.20)	-.22 (.17)	.08 (.12)	.44** (.17)	-.12 (.10)
Income	-.84 (.61)	-.13 (.64)	.30 (.48)	-.16 (.39)	.14 (.48)	.15 (.32)
Recipient Characteristics						
Geographic Proximity	-.19+ (.10)	-.05 (.08)	.19* (.08)	-.01 (.05)	-.08 (.08)	.06 (.04)
Health	.13 (.13)	-.12 (.10)	.13 (.10)	.06 (.06)	-.18+ (.10)	-.01 (.05)
Income	-.14 (.18)	-.05 (.17)	-.24+ (.14)	-.15 (.10)	-.11 (.14)	.23** (.09)
Closeness	.31* (.15)	.09 (.10)	.06 (.12)	.14** (.06)	-.04 (.12)	-.01 (.05)
Marriage	-.16 (.27)	-.19 (.20)	.25 (.21)	-.08 (.12)	.17 (.21)	.07 (.10)
Gender	.18 (.27)	.07 (.25)	-.01 (.21)	.01 (.15)	-.20 (.21)	.14 (.12)
Constant	1.04+ (.57)	.87+ (.53)	-.35 (.44)	.39 (.32)	.64 (.44)	-.25 (.27)
R^2	.39* (.61)	.05 (.87)	.28 (.48)	.12 (.53)	.26 (.48)	.28** (.44)

Notes: Unstandardized beta coefficients (ß). Significance levels: $+\leq.10$; $*\leq.05$; $**\leq.01$; $***\leq.001$. Standard error in parentheses. See notes, Table 5.2, for a description of these variables. Number of friends helped by men=44, by women=107.

types of tasks on the characteristics of those receiving care. In general, the help older men give friends is more consistently affected by the friends' needs than is the help given by older women. Older men give more material help to friends who are in poorer health than to friends who are in better health, while friends' health has no effect on any type of help from older women. Older men also give more personal help to friends with lower income, while friends with lower income receive less, not more, material help from older women.[5]

These data clearly contradict the hypothesis that older women's helping friends is characterized by a greater responsiveness to the needs of others. At the same time, however, these data do not provide much support for the alternative hypothesis, that homogeneity of gender plays an important role in shaping the help older men and women give friends. Neither older men's nor older women's help to friends is significantly affected by friends' gender. Although homogeneity of gender status may play an important role in shaping interaction with friends, it is not significant in predicting the amount or type of help either older men or older women provide.

What *do* affect the help older men and women give friends are friends' characteristics that facilitate giving care: geographic proximity and affective closeness. As with characteristics reflecting relative need for help, characteristics that facilitate giving care are more frequently significant for older men than for older women. Geographic proximity, for example, significantly affects the practical and personal help older men give friends but has no effect on the types of help older women provide.

Affective closeness, on the other hand, is no more often significant for older men than for older women. Yet the effects of emotional closeness differ across types of help and support. Older men give more practical help to friends to whom they feel more close than to friends to whom they feel less close. For older women, closeness matters for personal support, but not for practical or material help and support. Older women give more personal help to friends to whom they feel more close; but closeness does not effect the practical and material support older women give friends.

Overall, then, more kinds of help from older men are significantly affected by friends' material and social needs, as well their geographic and affective closeness, than is help from older women. Because older men give significantly less help to friends than do older women, this suggests older men help friends in response to particular needs, or within the context of particularly close friendships. Older women's help to friends, on the other hand, may consist of more frequent (and more time consuming) expressions of "neighborliness" that reinforce friendship and neighborhood ties, rather than help given in response to friends' needs for significant care.

SUMMARY AND DISCUSSION

Three points should be emphasized in summarizing these findings. First, the kinds of help both older women and older men give adult children are shaped by characteristics reflecting children's needs, as well as characteristics that facilitate giving care. Both older men and women give care. What they provide, and to whom they give it, however, are responsive to different circumstances. The help older women give adult children appears to be linked to children's financial need slightly more than is the case for older men. However, this effect is limited to personal support from mothers to daughters and does not appear for practical or material support to either daughters or sons—suggesting a lack of access to or control over the financial resources within marriage with which these women might meet the material needs of an adult child.

While children's finances may have little effect on the help older men provide, the help older men give adult children is more closely linked to adult children's health than is the help older women provide. In general, then, older women's care is no more linked to children's needs than is older men's. Rather, women and men respond to different types of needs with different types of help and support. These findings help to specify those of other work on parent-child relations (Rossi and Rossi, 1990)—where helping adult children differs not only with the gender and marital status of the adult child, but across types of help and support as well.

Third, looking at care given to friends: the help older men give friends is more closely linked to the health and financial status of those they help than in older women's. Although this relationship is not very strong, it suggests that if an ethic of care is to be found in helping friends in need, that ethic is slightly more characteristic of older men than of older women.

The findings of this chapter provide only minimal support for the hypothesis that gender differences in older people's giving care reflect more fundamental differences between men and women. The help older women give family and friends is generally no more, and no less, linked to the needs of those they help than is older men's. The help older women give family and friends is more characterized by an ethic of care than is older men's. Nor do these data provide much support for the alternative hypothesis—that homogeneity of gender, more than the need of the recipient, shapes the care given by older women and men.

Finally, it is important to note that older women's care is more responsive to the needs of the recipient only in terms of more personal help to daughters who are in greater financial need. Older women's "difference," then, extends primarily to the comfort and advice they give family, especially daughters, rather than friends. Older women's ethic of care, to the extent that it is an extension of their mothering, does not extend much past the relations in which they are literally mothers. And, as I discuss in the next chapter, it extends even less to those in need who are neither family nor friends.

NOTES

1. While there is some advantage to using hours of help as an indicator of the depth of care given, data were collected on hours of help to categories of recipients (i.e., parents, parents-in-law, or adult children) rather than individual recipients.

2. Thus far, the unit of analysis has been the individual providing care. In this chapter the unit of analysis shifts to the individual being helped. The primary question here is, How do the characteristics of individual recipients affect the help given by older men and women?, rather than, How do the characteristics of older people affect the number of individuals, types of help, or amount of time spent helping others?

3. The coefficients for the effects of daughter's marriage on the practical and material help older mothers provide are also positive. This is not the case for the effects of children's marriage on other types of help from fathers. Although they are not significant, they suggest that the help older women give daughters may be linked not only to daughters' needs as individuals but to the needs of daughters' husbands, and (in most cases) children—who either directly or indirectly increase maternal care. While there may be some inflation of care to adult children through combining help to a child's spouse with help to a child, this effect is probably fairly small. Most respondents were careful to distinguish among help to an adult child, help to a child's spouse, and help to both. Interviewers were also careful to probe for specific recipients of care, asking, "Did you do that for your son/daughter, or was it also for his/her spouse?" More frequently, the effects of daughters' marriage on the help older women give are probably more direct—increasing the amount of care mothers give through increasing daughters' need for help with domestic work, advice about work and family, and "opportunities" for child care.

4. Geographic proximity scores are coded from 0 for "in the same household" to 6 for "more than 2 hours away". The direction of the effect of proximity on help provided is consistently negative—indicating that children who live closer to their mothers and fathers receive more support than those who live farther away.

5. This somewhat anomalous finding may reflect older women's giving friends material help in the form of everyday gifts or loans of money or goods, rather than larger, more substantial gifts given specifically to meet a financial need.

6

Gender and Giving Help through Formal Volunteerism

BACKGROUND

Just as gender shapes the help older men and women give family and friends, it also affects help given to others in need—others helped through older men's and women's formal volunteer efforts. Gender differences in volunteering reflect economic and domestic roles, as much as they may reflect a greater sense of connectedness and responsibility for others among women. Previous research finds men tend to belong to slightly more volunteer groups than do women (Babchuk and Booth, 1969; Booth, 1972; Curtis, 1971; Scott, 1957), especially more job oriented and fraternal groups (Booth, 1972; McPherson and Smith-Lovin, 1982). Women, on the other hand, generally belong to fewer groups, but spend more time volunteering than men—especially in service, religious and youth oriented groups (Booth, 1972; McPherson and Smith-Lovin, 1982).

Among the elderly, for whom employment and child rearing are largely past, these differences are muted as older men and women adopt new social and economic roles. Volunteerism itself may substitute for the loss of paid labor for men, and the loss of the wife/homemaker role for women (Cohen and Gans, 1978). To the extent that this is the case, we would expect retired older men to spend more time in community volunteer associations (though less in work related organizations) than their still-employed counterparts. If so, gender differences in providing care through formal volunteer efforts may be less apparent among the elderly for the simple reason that more of them are retired. Yet a number of studies argue that this is not the case. Men's participation in volunteer associations tends to decline, rather than increase, after retirement (Chambre, 1984; Riley and Foner, 1968). Nor does retirement significantly reduce the gender gap in volunteering. Retired men are 45 percent less likely to volunteer than employed men; while retired women volunteer 25 percent less than employed women (Chambre, 1984).[1]

While there is some question as to the effects of retirement on the number of groups older men join, or amount of time they volunteer, retirement does seem to be accompanied by a shift in the *types* of groups to which older men belong. A summary of research conducted in the 1960s suggests that participation in volunteer groups shifts from business related associations to more social/recreational organizations (Riley and Foner, 1968). To the extent that this is still the case, retired men may be particularly *unlikely* to provide the types of community service or charity work currently encouraged by the state.

HYPOTHESES

Because the larger context of most sociological research on volunteerism is the social participation of the elderly, rather than the giving of care, we know relatively little about the ways in which gender shapes the types or amount of help older people give through volunteer associations. Nor do we know the ways in which competing demands for care from family and friends shape older men's and women's volunteer efforts. This chapter examines a number of hypotheses related to these issues.

First, I examine three broad indicators of volunteerism: likelihood of participating in any sort of formal volunteer group, total number of group memberships, and hours of participation. On the basis of the finding of little gender difference in the number of friends helped (care that is voluntary), as well as the findings of previous research, we might expect that gender has little effect on these measures of volunteerism. More specifically, we might expect older men to be as likely to volunteer, belong to a similar number of volunteer organizations, and spend a similar amount of time volunteering as older women.

Next, the focus narrows to volunteerism that is intended to help the needy—the kind of traditional charity work being encouraged by the state. Because older women's informal help to family and friends does not tend to be more responsive to the characteristics of the recipients than is older men's, we might expect gender to have little effect on care given to needy others through volunteerism. More specifically, older men may be as likely as older women to participate in volunteer organizations that help the needy and, when employment is controlled for, to spend similar amounts of time helping the needy as do older women.

Third, we look more specifically at the types of groups and kinds of work older men and women do as volunteers. Work and family roles may affect the types of groups to which older men and women belong. Employment, in particular, may draw older men into economically oriented groups, at the same time that it limits the hours available for other types of volunteering. Moreover, to the extent that men's volunteerism is an extension of their business and economic interests (expanding networks, and establishing status and reputation), the types of work older men do as volunteers may differ from specific tasks older women do. I expect older men to be active in managing volunteer activities and participating in activities that promote the groups to which they belong (such as letter writing or lobbying), and older women to be more involved in providing direct care to those in need, and in performing supportive services within volunteer organizations. If gender differences in the types of groups or types of tasks done by older volunteers disappear when employment is constant, it would suggest that economic interests (rather than innate differences in nurturing and care) play an important role in shaping the work older men and women do as volunteers.

Finally, I examine the links between informal help to family and friends and help given others through formal volunteer efforts. These links may have two, very different sets of effects on older men's and women's volunteerism. On the one hand, because time and energy are finite resources, competing demands for care from family and friends may reduce the amount of time older men and women spend helping others. On the other hand, because helping family and friends provides some indication of social participation, greater involvement in helping family and friends may spill over into greater involvement in helping others as well.

ANALYSIS

At the most basic level, the majority of both older men and women belong to at least one volunteer association (Table 6.1). In fact, the percentages of older men and older women who belong to at least one volunteer group are almost the same: 69 percent of the older men and 67 percent of the older women.

Older women, however, spend slightly (but not significantly) more time volunteering than do older men. On average, older men spend 9 ½ hours a month volunteering   only about an hour less than older women. Older men also belong to a greater number of groups than do older women (approximately 3 groups for men and 2 groups for women; $p \leq .10$).

These findings are generally consistent with those of previous research, that older men belong to a larger number of volunteer associations, but spend less time volunteering than do older women. Using regression analysis, it is possible to control for the effects employment has on these basic indicators of volunteerism among older men and women. In addition to employment, I control for the effects of other variables previous research indicates are predictors of volunteerism. These are higher family income,[2] age, self-reported physical health, and race, as well as a measure of significant involvement in helping others in the past (history of being "caregivers"). In addition, variables are included to assess the effects of hours of care to family and friends on hours of volunteering. The results of this analysis are shown in Table 6.2.

Table 6.1
Volunteerism Among Older Men and Women
(t-Tests)

	Men	Women
Any Groups (% yes)	.69 (.47)	.67(.47)
Total Groups (mean #)	3.03 (3.46)	2.13 (2.17)+
Hours Volunteering (mean #)	9.54 (14.27)	10.48 (18.15)

Notes: Symbols indicate level of significance based on a chi-square for belonging to any groups, and on a one-tailed t-Test for number of groups and hours of volunteering (per month): $+\leq.10$; $*\leq.05$; $**\leq.01$; $***\leq.001$. Standard deviations in parentheses. Men, N=32; women, N=55.

As expected, when we control for the effects of other variables that contribute to caregiving resources as well as compete for them, gender does not significantly predict either number of volunteer group memberships or hours of participation. Somewhat surprisingly, neither does employment. Instead, better health increases hours of volunteering, and both better health and greater income increase the number of groups to which both older men and women belong. In general, these findings suggest that resources—higher income and better health—affect participation in volunteer associations more than gender itself.

When we look at competing demands for care, neither hours of help to friends, nor hours of help to family significantly affect group membership or hours of volunteering. Still, the direction of the association is consistent with the expectation that help to family and friends represents a competing demand for care that might be given to others.

Gender and Helping the Needy

If a greater ethic of care exists among women, we might expect to find evidence for it in volunteering to help the needy, more than in volunteerism in general. Table 6.3 compares older men's and women's volunteering to help different types of needy: the poor, sick, elderly and other groups.

More than half of older men, as well as half of older women, participate in some volunteer activity that helps the needy. Contrary to what might be expected, older men are slightly *more* likely than older women to volunteer to

Table 6.2
OLS Regression of Number of Groups and Hours of Volunteering on Gender, Age, Health, Income, Employment, History of Help, and Race

Respondent Characteristics	Number of Groups	Hours of Volunteering[a]
Gender[b]	.57 (.62)	-.80 (4.36)
Age	.03 (.05)	.19 (.34)
Health	-.93 ** (.34)	-6.27** (2.41)
Income[c]	.47 ** (1.60)	.68 (11.14)
History of Help	.06 (.10)	.69 (.68)
Race	-.06 (.69)	-7.25 (4.87)
Employment[d]	.66 (.62)	.06 (4.40)
Care to Family[e]	.31 (.43)	-3.88 (3.05)
Care to Friends[e]	3.43 (2.80)	-5.28 (19.85)
Constant	-.48 (3.40)	7.98 (24.07)
R^2	.36 *** (2.43)	.14 (16.40)

Note: Unstandardized beta coefficients (ß). Symbols indicate significance levels: $+\leq.10$; $*\leq.05$; $**\leq.01$; $***\leq.001$. Standard errors in parentheses. Men, N=32; women, N=55. [a] Hours volunteering per month. [b] Men=1; women=0. [c] Family income in dollars, x 10,000. [d] Employed: yes=1; no=0. [e] Hours per month helping family and friends x 100.

Table 6.3
Older Men's and Women's Charity Work
(t-Tests)

I. Percent Who Help	Men	Women
The Poor	.56 (1.37)	.58 (1.30)
The Sick	.66 (1.23)	.55 (1.27)
The Elderly	.72 (1.25)	.58 (1.26)
Other Needy	.78 (1.85)	.60 (1.33)
The Poor, Sick, Elderly or Other Needy People[b]	1.13 (1.85)	1.02 (1.58)
II. Hours Helping		
The Poor	53.06 (135.59)	54.15 (147.39)
The Sick	62.94 (129.66)	46.20 (127.94)
The Elderly	52.47 (120.23)	47.22 (128.84)
Other Needy	62.56 (140.50)	53.35 (145.11)
The Poor, Sick, Elderly, or Other Needy People[c]	81.50 (145.65)	85.95 (189.50)

Notes: Level of significance: $+ \leq .10$; $* \leq .05$; $** \leq .01$; $*** \leq .001$. Men, N=32; women, N=55. [a] Since each group may help more than one type of needy person, mean scores may be greater than 1. [b] Hours spent last year helping each group of needy persons may overlap (e.g., hours to poor may also have been hours to the sick).

help the poor, old, sick or other needy. Older men also spend slightly more time than older women participating in volunteer groups that help the needy. However, none of these differences is statistically significant.

In fact, when variables contributing to older men's and women's abilities to help others are controlled for, the only significant predictor of help to the needy is race (Table 6.4). Even controlling for family income, older men and women who are black spend an average of 85 hours more per year—more than 7 hours a month—helping others in need than do older men and women who are white.

Table 6.4
OLS Regression of Hours of Charity Work on Gender, Age, Health, Income, History of Help, Employment and Race

	Poor	Sick	Elderly	Other
Gender	6.54 (39.06)	17.73 (34.36)	9.40 (33.60)	-4.76 (37.59)
Age	-1.72 (3.02)	-.95 (2.66)	-1.24 (2.60)	.63 (2.91)
Health	-16.83 (21.64)	-25.92 (19.03)	-28.70 (18.61)	-22.98 (20.82)
Income	4.91 (101.85)	1.73 (89.57)	5.92 (87.60)	15.59 (98.00)
History of Help	6.74 (6.10)	6.89 (5.36)	4.99 (5.24)	-1.64 (5.87)
Race	-9.53 (43.66)	30.11 (38.40)	-1.89 (37.55)	-85.40 (42.01)*
Employment	-10.21 (39.46)	.36 (34.70)	-18.04 (33.93)	-1.39 (37.97)
Controls:				
Care to Kin	-8.09 (27.36)	-23.38 (24.06)	-23.73 (23.53)	-40.36 (26.33)
Care to Friends	-13.98 (17.88)	-7.29 (156.44)	7.85 (15.30)	118.22 (17.11)
Constant	168.59 (215.65)	99.25 (189.65)	149.65 (185.46)	86.92 (207.50)
R^2	.05 (147.00)	.09 (129.28)	.09 (126.43)	.12 (141.45)

Notes: Hours of volunteering last year with groups that help the needy. Unstandardized beta coefficients (ß). Symbols indicate significance levels: $+\leq.10$; $*\leq.05$; $**\leq.01$; $***\leq.001$. Standard errors in parentheses. N=87. See Table 6.2 for a description of these independent variables.

Along with the significance of race, it is important to point out the *lack* of significance of gender in predicting hours of charity work. When it comes to the amount of time spent volunteering in groups that help the needy, older men and women do not significantly differ. In fact, the direction of the relationship between gender and hours of charity work indicates that, if anything, older men may spend *more* time helping the needy than do older women.

A lack of gender difference in hours of charity work contradicts the image of traditional women volunteers—devoted to helping those in need, whether poor, sick, or elderly. Just as older men and women do not significantly differ in helping family and friends according to their needs, neither do older men and women significantly differ in the amount of time they devote to helping needy strangers through the work they do as volunteers.

Gender and the Tasks Involved in Volunteering

If gender does not affect older men's and women's involvement in traditional charity work, perhaps it does affect the types of specific tasks they do as volunteers. This section focuses on highly involved volunteers—those who spend 50 hours or more per year working with a particular volunteer association. In spite of the image of women's volunteerism as an extension of their mothering into the community, a greater proportion of older men are highly involved as volunteers: 43.8 percent of the older men, but only 32.7 percent of the older women fall into this category. Although this difference is not significant at conventional levels, the small number of cases on which the comparison is based (N=32) may miss significant effects a larger sample, with a higher level of statistical power, might reveal.

Table 6.5 shows that older men are slightly more likely than older women to give direct care to those in need, to act as treasurer, supervise volunteers, do fund-raising, write letters, recruit members or perform other tasks. In contrast, older women are slightly more likely than older men to organize meetings, act as speakers, preside over meetings, or do secretarial work. Both older men and older women are similarly involved in telephoning for the groups with which they are highly involved.

Two points are important here—both related to the absence of gender difference in performing specific group tasks. First, there is no clear pattern wherein older men are more likely to participate in leadership roles within volunteer organizations than are older women. Second, not only do the tasks older men and women volunteers perform not follow conventional gender roles, there are also no significant differences between older men and older women on any of the tasks they may perform as volunteers.

Table 6.5
Tasks Older Men and Women Perform for High Involvement Groups
(t-Tests)

Task	Percent who do each task	
	Men	Women
Direct Care	.50 (.52)	.39 (.50)
Treasurer	.14 (.36)	.06 (.24)
Supervise Volunteers	.36 (.50)	.28 (.46)
Fund Raising	.29 (.47)	.17 (.38)
Organize Meetings	.21 (.43)	.22 (.43)
Speaker	.29 (.47)	.33 (.49)
Presider	.14 (.36)	.17 (.38)
Write Letters	.21 (.43)	.06 (.24)
Recruit Members	.36 (.50)	.33 (.49)
Secretary	.14 (.36)	.17 (.38)
Telephone	.50 (.52)	.50 (.51)
Other	.07 (.27)	.06 (.24)

Notes: Symbols indicate level of significance: $+\leq.10$; $*\leq.05$; $**\leq.01$; $***\leq.001$. Men, N=32; women, N=55. All figures are per month for highly involved men and women (e.g., those volunteering 50+hours per year for a particular volunteer group).

It is only when the effects of variables influencing older men's and women's ability to perform these tasks are held constant that gender appears as a significant predictor of group tasks—and that only for fund-raising (data not shown). There, older men do fund-raising for significantly more groups than older women. Gender has no significant effect on any other type of task older men and women do as highly involved volunteers. Together, these findings provide little support for the hypothesis that older women's volunteerism is characterized by greater services and support to those in need.

The Effects of Gender on Types of Groups

Although gender does not significantly affect the types of work older men and women do as volunteers, previous research does suggest that significant gender differences exist in the types of groups to which men and women belong. These differences may reflect men's economic and women's nurturing and domestic roles, as well as access to greater resources such as higher income or better health.

Older men and women do significantly differ in the types of groups to which they belong. Older men belong to significantly more job oriented groups (.05 versus .06, p<. 05), more veterans groups (.31 versus .11, p<.10), and more political groups (.56 versus .16, p<.10), as well as more service and fraternal groups (.31 versus .06, p<.01), than do older women. This is consistent with the hypothesis that men's volunteerism reflects their economic and political interests. Older women, on the other hand, belong to significantly more religious groups than do older men (.58 versus .19, p<.01). However, no significant gender differences appear in the number of welfare groups, youth groups, groups for the elderly, recreational groups, community groups or arts/cultural groups to which older men and women belong.

These findings are generally consistent with those of previous research. However, they provide only weak support for the hypothesis that the help women give through formal volunteerism reflects a greater ethic of care than does older men's. In fact, for most types of groups (particularly welfare groups) we find no evidence of a greater ethic of care among older women.

More importantly, when the competing demands of employment, hours of help to family, and hours of help to friends are controlled for, most of these gender differences disappear (Table 6.6). In fact, it is only for groups whose memberships are almost entirely male—veterans groups and service groups (such as the Fraternal Order of the Elks or the Rotary Club)—that older men are significantly more involved than are older women. In these cases, older men belong to groups which are clearly related to their economic and political interests. Higher family income—and not gender—also significantly increases both older men's and older women's membership in welfare, youth, job, political, and cultural groups.

Two points are important here. First, what appears to be a significant gender difference in belonging to job and politically oriented groups is actually more an effect of income than of gender. Access to material resources—for both older women and older men—significantly increases participation in groups which serve economic and political purposes.

Second, what appears to be a significant gender difference in belonging to religious organizations is more closely linked to one's history of giving care than to one's gender. Both older men and women who have been active in providing significant help to others in the past belong to more religious groups than their

Table 6.6
OLS Regression of Types of Groups on Gender, Age, Health, Income, History of Help, Employment, and Race

	Welfare	Youth	Job	Veterans	Elderly	Political
Gender	-.03 (.18)	-.01 (.07)	.25 (.21)	.29 (.16)+	.00 (.18)	.21 (.27)
Age	-.01 (.01)	.00 (.01)	-.01 (.02)	-.01 (.01)	.02 (.01)	-.02 (.02)
Health	-.16 (.10)+	-.03 (.04)	-.06 (.12)	-.00 (.09)	-.04 (.10)	-.18 (.15)
Income	1.14 (.46)*	.42 (.18)*	1.10 (.54)*	.31 (.41)	.23 (.46)	1.44 (.70)*
History of Help	-.01 (.03)	.02 (.01)	-.01 (.03)	.01 (.03)	.04 (.03)	-.02 (.04)
Race	-.05 (.20)	-.20 (.08)	.10 (.23)	-.27 (.18)	.18 (.20)	.14 (.30)
Employment	-.08 (.18)	-.03 (.07)	.18 (.21)	-.09 (.16)	.10 (.18)	.13 (.27)
Controls:						
Care to Kin	-.08 (.12)	.03 (.01)	-.05 (.14)	-.05 (.11)	-.13 (.12)	.07 (.19)
Care to Friends	2.52 (.80)**	.11 (.31)	-1.00 (.95)	1.60 (.72)*	1.46 (.80)+	-1.66 (1.22)
Constant	.47 (.98)	.04 (.38)	.37 (1.15)	.53 (.87)	-1.34 (.97)	1.19 (1.48)
R^2	.33 (.66)***	.19 (.26)*	.20 (.78)*	.13 (.59)	.14 (.66)	.21 (1.10)*

Notes: Unstandardized beta coefficients (ß). Symbols indicate significance levels: +$\leq$.10; *$\leq$.05; **$\leq$.01; ***$\leq$.001. N=87. See Table 6.2 for a description of these variables.

Table 6.6
(Continued)

	Ethnic	Service	Religious	Recreation	Community	Art/ Cultural
Gender	-.01 (.07)	.24 (.10)*	-.28 (.19)	.02 (.11)	-.02 (.05)	-.10 (.07)
Age	.01 (.01)	.01 (.01)	.02 (.01)	.00 (.01)	-.00 (.00)	.00 (.01)
Health	.04 (.04)	-.00 (.06)	-.29 (.11)**	-.11 (.06)+	-.03 (.03)	-.06 (.04)
Income	.15 (.19)	.11 (.26)	-.62 (.50)	-.21 (.29)	.17 (.12)	.41 (.18)*
History of Help	.01 (.01)	.02 (.02)	-.04 (.03)	.06 (.02)**	.02 (.01)*	-.02 (.01)*
Race	-.05 (.08)	.01 (.11)	.02 (.21)	.15 (.12)	-.06 (.05)	-.02 (.08)
Employment	.11 (.07)	-.01 (.10)	.07 (.19)	.09 (.11)	.02 (.05)	.01 (.07)
Controls:						
Care to Kin	-.05 (.05)	-.03 (.07)	.06 (.13)	-.08 (.08)	-.03 (.03)	-.07 (.05)
Care to Friends	-.34 (.33)	-.13 (.46)	1.39 (.87)	-.62 (.51)	-.18 (.22)	.29 (.32)
Constant	-.50 (.40)	-.86 (.55)	-.27 (1.06)	-.06 (.62)	.08 (.26)	-.11 (.39)
R²	.10 (.28)	.16 (.39)	.22 (.72)*	.20 (.42)*	.14 (.18)	.19 (.27)*

Notes: Unstandardized beta coefficients (β). Symbols indicate significance levels: +≤.10; *≤.05; **≤.01; ***≤.001. N=87. See Table 6.2 for a description of these variables.

less involved counterparts. Overall, then, if an ethic of care is to be found in the types of groups to which older men and women belong, it is a gender neutral ethic of care reflecting a long history of helping others.

Finally, neither employment nor competing demands of caring for kin affect the particular types of volunteering older men and women do. This is not the case, however, when we examine the effects of involvement in helping friends on volunteerism.

Links between Formal Volunteerism and Informal Care

While neither hours of care to family nor hours of care to friends significantly affect the number of groups, hours of help, or types of tasks older men and women do as volunteers, hours of care to friends *do* affect the types of groups to which older men and women belong (see Table 6.6). Contrary to the hypotheses that help to friends reduces volunteerism, we find that the more time older men and women spend helping friends, the greater the number of welfare, veterans, and elderly groups to which they belong. This suggests an important link between helping friends and helping others—one that older men and women frequently commented on as they discussed their participation in formal volunteer activities.

As they discussed their history and motivations for volunteering, a number of older people indicated they had joined volunteer groups specifically because a friend had encouraged them to do so. As one woman explained:

> When my age group was young and our children were from cradle on up to junior high age, we stayed home and we took care of them. We did a lot of volunteer work then. A lot! Most of us quit volunteering after we started workin—we just didn't have the energy. Now most of us have retired. I never missed them when they were working and I was home puttering with the flowers, but now that they're retiring too and beginning to volunteer again. Whatever they do, I'll do, just because I enjoy them.

Sometimes invitations to volunteer are related to particular times of personal crisis or loss. In these cases, volunteering is most clearly a substitute for lost family or work roles—as in the case of a 69 year-old retired woman who explained how a friend encouraged her to volunteer after the death of her daughter. "After my daughter died, one of my friends called and asked me to get involved in the nursing home ministry through our church. I did, and I think it helped me get back into things." In some cases, then, volunteering serves as a coping device that also serves the greater social good.

At the same time, while friends may invite participation in volunteer associations, the response is certainly not always immediately positive. Older people who are in poorer health, in particular, may initially resist friend's invitations to join volunteer associations, as a woman who was still hesitating explained. "My neighbor wants me to go to meetings for disabled veterans, but I don't know. The meetings are in the evenings and I'm usually tired by then." But, after pausing, she continued, "But I think I may start going."

In some cases, then, friends draw older men and women into volunteer groups. In general, however, this seemed to be true more for older women than for older men. Older women frequently linked their involvement as volunteers to their existing friendships with other women, while older men less commonly made this connection. In contrast, the link between friendship and volunteerism more often seemed to work in the other direction for older men—as they joined groups specifically to make friends, whether for social, political, or economic reasons. One retired man explained the importance of his joining a local volunteer group as a young man, recently emigrated from Quebec: "When I came to this country, I didn't know anyone. They said if you belong to that club, they will help you. So I joined. I thought it would be good for me to get to meet some people, and they said it (would) keep me out of trouble with the police." That the intent of his joining was explicitly to make friends, as well and keep out of trouble, perhaps as an illegal immigrant, was made clear in that, when he felt he had *not* made friends, he quit the organization: "I'd go, but they were all strangers. I never knew that many, and the one I knew was not at the meeting that week or that month, so it didn't mean that much to me. So I stopped going after a while."

In some cases, then, volunteering does not successfully link men and women to larger networks of friends. Yet, in most cases it does—as reflected in the ways in which most older men and women responded when asked whether volunteering had cut down on the time they would like to spend with friends. Over 90 percent of the women and 84 percent of the men said volunteering had not decreased the time they would like to spend with their friends at all. Instead, both older men and older women frequently explained that volunteering was a way for them to spend *more* time with their friends, responding, "Not at all, because the people I do it with are my friends" or "My friends are all there."

In these ways, both quantitative and qualitative data suggest that helping friends and neighbors and helping others through volunteer associations are linked—each providing access and opportunity to extend care to the other.

SUMMARY AND DISCUSSION

Several points should be emphasized in summarizing these findings. First, gender plays at most a minimal role in shaping patterns of help older people give through formal volunteerism. It is only in belonging to typically male dominated groups—veterans or fraternal and service groups—and in doing more fund-raising that gender makes a difference, and there, older men do more, not less, than older women.

Second, and perhaps more important, gender makes no difference in care given through volunteer associations to those in need who are neither family nor friends. Since helping others through volunteer associations is by definition care that older men and women are not obligated to provide, it would seem that gender makes the least difference in care that is most and least obligatory—care to kin who are related by blood (Chapter 4) and care given to strangers through volunteer associations. Also, just as older women's informal help is no more linked to the needs of those they help than is older men's, neither are older women more involved in formal volunteerism that helps others in need than are older men. These findings clearly do not support the hypothesis that patterns of help reflect a greater ethic of care among women than among men.

Third, rather than gender, what does appear to affect help given through formal volunteer associations are older men's and women's personal resources—particularly higher income and better health, but also greater history of helping others. Greater material and physical resources, as well as greater experience in helping others in the past, increase the amount of time spent in volunteer work and number of groups to which both older men and older women belong. However, even higher income and better health have very limited effects on the hours older men and women spend in volunteer activities that specifically help the needy. It seems, then, that older men and women who volunteer to help others persist in doing so in spite of limited physical and material resources—suggesting, as was pointed out a number of years ago, that older volunteers are volunteers who have aged (Dye et al., 1973).

Fourth, these findings also suggest the importance of linking formal and informal care. In particular, greater involvement in caring for friends actually increases, rather than decreases, care given to strangers. Friends draw both older men and women into volunteer groups. So, too, participation in these groups provides greater opportunity for helping friends   as well as others in need.

Finally, these findings have important implications for both theories of care and public policy aimed at increasing volunteerism among the elderly. The lack of gender difference revealed by this analysis suggests that older men's and women's help is shaped by economic and political interests and resources, more than a distinctly female ethic of care. Men's and women's participation in formal volunteer efforts reflects not women's greater connectedness or sense of responsibility to others, but the persistence of gendered adult roles as breadwinners, as wives and mothers, and as volunteers.

NOTES

1. Types of volunteer associations included are health (hospital, mental health clinic, fund-raising drives, etc.); education (teacher's aide, tutor, etc.), justice (court volunteers, legal aids, etc.); citizenship (scout leader, VFW officer, etc.); recreation (activity leader, Little League coach, etc.); social and welfare (homes for the aged, orphanages, etc.); civic and community (environmental, consumer, etc.); religious (usher, choir, Sunday school teacher, etc.); political (fund-raiser, poll watcher, campaign worker, etc.), and other (ACTION, 1975).

2. Family income, rather than personal income, is used here for two reasons. First, most of the older married women in this sample (75 percent) are not currently employed. These are coded as having zero personal income. Using personal income, then, would underestimate the economic resources available to older women as volunteers. Second, to the extent that personal income is a function of employment, it provides little additional explanation for differences in older men's and women's volunteering.

Part III

Marriage, Widowhood
and Giving Care

Several findings in Part II suggest that women's roles as wives significantly affect the help they give others—whether informal help to family or friends or help to others through formal volunteer associations. Marriage seems to draw women into sets of caring relationships in a way that it does not men. Older women's caring, then, may be shaped as much by marriage, by being wives, as by gender itself. In this section, we turn from gender to marriage and examine the ways in which married and widowed women differ in the help and support they give others.

BACKGROUND

Previous research contains some evidence that marriage does indeed affect older women's care. Most analyses, however, focus primarily on help received—rather than given—and on women in general rather than older women in particular. Still, findings from this research raise important issues regarding the role of marriage in shaping patterns of interaction and obligation between women and their family and friends—patterns which may also be reflected in the care they provide.

In particular, scholars argue that marriage both isolates women and integrates them into larger networks of family, friends and others. On the one hand, some argue that marriage is "greedy"—that it is socially isolating and limits helping networks (Altergott, 1985; Coser and Coser, 1974; Gerstel, 1988). Others, on the other hand, argue that marriage integrates women into larger networks of family and friends and provides greater opportunity for giving care (Fischer, 1982; O'Donnell, 1985).

The findings in Chapter 4 seem to provide more support for the argument that marriage integrates women into larger social networks—networks that involve providing help and support to a wide range of relatives, as well as friends and neighbors. However, rather than simply focusing on married women versus married men, this section extends the analysis begun in Part II and compares patterns of help among widows and wives. It examines both sides of marriage: marriage as an integrator and marriage as an isolator of women's helping efforts. To the extent that marriage is socially isolating, widowhood may afford women new opportunities for building relationships—relationships which include giving of help and support—with family, friends and others. On the other hand, to the extent that marriage is socially integrating, loss of a spouse may result in a decline in relationships with others, including relations in which older women help others.

At the same time, marriage certainly does not operate independently of other social characteristics in shaping older women's care. Because marriage is associated with higher family income, it may provide older women with greater material resources for helping others, at the same time that it increases obligations to help those in need. Along with marriage, then, this section also examines the effects of older women's material resources on the help they give family and friends. In addition, controls are included for the effects of older women's physical resources—their age and health—on older women's caring.

Finally, marriage may also affect the ways in which the help older women give is linked to different "demands" for care—to the needs of those they help. On the one hand, married women's greater material resources may result in wives' care being more responsive to the needs of others than is widowed women's. Yet, as the findings in Chapter 5 suggest, married women may have limited control over how their material resources are used in helping others. As a result, widowed women's care may be more—rather than less—linked to the needs of others than is married women's.

The following three chapters address these issues. Chapter 7 focuses on the ways in which marriage shapes the informal help older widows and wives give to family and friends. In Chapter 8, I extend that analysis, and look in detail at the ways in which the characteristics of the recipients affect older widows' and wives' informal help to family and friends. Finally I turn to formal help in Chapter 9 and examine the effects of marriage on older women's participation in volunteer associations.

7

Marriage and Informal Help
to Family and Friends

BACKGROUND

Some have argued that marriage integrates women into larger networks—particularly with kin—and provides greater opportunities for helping both family and friends. The image of the "integrated" married woman may be part of what contributes to the stereotype of widowhood as being filled with loneliness and isolation. The assumption behind this image of widowhood is that marriage is an essential link between women and their families and friends. When women are no longer married, these ties presumably dwindle and die. From these images, we might assume married women would be clearly more involved in giving care than widows.

In sharp contrast is the image of marriage as a "greedy" institution (Coser and Coser, 1974)—one whose rights over the time, energies, and resources of its members take precedence over nearly all others. In particular, marriage as a greedy institution restricts women's relationships with those outside the nuclear family. To the extent that this is the case, if there are isolated women, they may be found less among widows than among wives.

Marriage, then, may have very contradictory effects on older women's giving care. While, on the one hand, marriage may integrate women into larger networks of family and friends to whom they provide care, it may also isolate women—focusing their care more on family than on friends. In this chapter, then, I begin to examine the ways in which older women's informal help to family and friends is shaped by whether they are married or widowed. Although very little previous research examines this question, there is some evidence that marriage does, indeed, shape older women's giving care. Moreover, there is some evidence that these effects vary for adult children, relatives in general, and friends and neighbors.

Helping Adult Children and Grandchildren

Most research on the effects of marriage on women's helping kin focuses on care provided to adult children and grandchildren. However, because previous research measures very limited aspects of women's caring or is often based on nonprobability samples, findings from these studies are somewhat contradictory. While not specifying the gender of the parent, Spitze and Logan (1992) find married parents give more regular help to adult children than do unmarried parents. Others find similar results for widows and wives: married women are more likely to provide more help to their adult children than widows (Lee and Ellithorpe, 1982). Still other research finds that the help older women give adult children (as well as grandchildren) is relatively unchanged by the loss of a spouse (Bankoff, 1984; Cherlin and Furstenberg, 1986; Hetherington, Cox and Cox, 1982).

There is greater consensus as to the ways in which marriage affects the types of support older women give their adult children. Overall, previous research finds widows give less financial and less practical support to adult children than do wives (L. A. Morgan, 1983; Rossi and Rossi, 1990). Some of this difference may be related to other social characteristics, rather than to marriage itself. Leslie Morgan (1983), for example, finds that lower family income among widows is more important than marital status in shaping the help older women give adult children. In addition, a greater history of giving help also increases women's involvement in giving care in old age (Brubaker, 1989; L. A. Morgan, 1983), as does being black—in spite of its correlation with lower income (Kivett, 1993; Malson, 1983; Mitchell and Register, 1984; L. A. Morgan, 1983). Somewhat surprisingly, health and general well-being do not appear to affect the amount of help women give their adult children (L. A. Morgan, 1983).

Helping Other Relatives

Less research focuses on the effects of marriage on helping other relatives. That which exists primarily emphasizes patterns of interaction rather than help and has produced somewhat contradictory results. Some studies find that widows interact less than wives with siblings and in-laws (Troll, Miller and Atchley, 1979; Lopata, 1978, 1973). Since most helping takes place within the context of interaction, we might expect widows to provide less help to these types of kin than do wives. Others, however, find widowhood has no significant effect on interaction with siblings (Waite and Harrison, 1992) and may even increase interaction with both siblings (Goetting, 1986) and other kin (Morgan, 1984). One possible explanation for these discrepant findings is the focus on different relatives. Widows, for example, may interact less with in-laws, but as much with their own kin as do their married counterparts. To the extent that this is the case, widowhood may involve a redistribution of care away from kin related by marriage toward kin related by blood.

Helping Friends and Neighbors

In response to a concern over the "isolated elderly," research on older women's friendships tends to focus primarily on the frequency of interaction rather than the content of that interaction. Early research on older women's friendships found that widows interact less than married women with friends (Berardo, 1968; Booth, 1972). More recent studies, however, find that widows interact at least as much, if not more, with friends as do still married women (Altergott, 1985; Babchuk and Anderson, 1989; Ferraro and Barresi, 1982; Rawlins, 1992).

Finally, scattered research suggests that marriage may also affect the *types* of help and support older women give to friends. Lopata (1973) argues that widows are a significant source of emotional and practical support for friends who are, themselves, recently widowed. For many of these women, widowhood provided greater opportunity for developing and maintaining friendships than had been possible while they were married. This is consistent with research on nonelderly populations that argues that marriage restricts women's ability to form and maintain relations with friends (Fischer, 1982; Gerstel, 1988; Rubin, 1985).

HYPOTHESES

Although it does little to specify the ways in which marriage might shape the amount, types or range of care older women provide, previous research suggests several hypotheses regarding the relationship between marriage and helping family and friends. First, to the extent that marriage is integrative, widowhood is likely to involve a narrowing of giving care. But that narrowing may be selective: widows may particularly turn to kin who are related by blood at the expense of those related by marriage. To the extent this is the case, we would expect declining ties to in-laws through the death of a spouse to result in greater help to one's own kin—adult children, grandchildren, and siblings.

Second, to the extent that marriage is "greedy"—a privatizing institution— widowhood may also involve a redistribution of care to nonkin. Thus we expect widowed women will provide more help and support to more friends than do women who are married.

Third, marriage does not act alone. Declining material and physical resources may reduce the amount and affect the types of care elderly women provide. Because marriage is associated with higher family income, it gives women greater material resources on which to draw in helping others. Thus, I control for the effects of family income on older women's care in the analysis. But I do not expect income to reduce all types of care equally. While widows may have lower income and, as a result, provide less material support, I also expect widowed women will provide at least as much labor intensive and emotional help and support as married women. In addition, I expect that women, both married and widowed, who are older and in poorer health will provide less care, to fewer people, than younger, healthier women. Thus, I control for these effects in the analysis. Finally, because blacks, and those with a history of giving care, may be especially likely to give aid, I assess the impact of these variables (and control for them) in the analysis.

ANALYSIS

Nearly all the women in this sample provided some type of help to at least one person (relative or friend) in the month prior to their interview. Ninety-six percent of the married women and 92 percent of the widows helped at least one person. While married women were slightly more likely to help a relative than were widows (93 versus 82 percent, p$\leq$.10), widows were slightly (but not significantly) more likely than wives to have helped a friend (75 versus 69 percent). Clearly, the majority of older women are not isolated and alone, but are involved in giving some sort of help to relatives and friends.

When we turn to the number of persons helped, we find that married women help almost twice the number of relatives (4.9 versus 2.6, p$\leq$.001), twice the number of their own kin (4 versus 2, p$\leq$.001), and twice the number of in-laws (.86 versus .45, p$\leq$.05) than do widows. In contrast, widows help a greater number of friends than do older married women (2.82 versus 1.95, p$\leq$.10). In addition, while we might expect that after the loss of a spouse, women would refocus their care on their own kin, we find no significant differences between married and widowed women in the proportion of kin helped who are related by marriage.

At this level, these data suggest that marriage integrates older women into networks of care. Overall, wives provide care to more people than do widows. Nevertheless, marriage is also privatizing. The people married women are more likely to help are relatives. In contrast, widows move outward—helping more neighbors and friends. In this sense, it is widowhood, not marriage, that is integrative.

A different picture emerges, however, when controls are introduced for those variables likely to affect giving care. Table 7.1 shows the results of regression analysis of the number of persons helped, controlling for material (family income), physical (age and health), and temporal (employment) resources, as well as prior history of help and race. In addition, we control for the presence of

Table 7.1
OLS Regression of Number of Persons Helped on Marriage, Age, Health, Income, History of Help, Race, and Employment

	Total Persons	# Kin	# Own Kin	# In-Laws	# Friends
Marriage[a]	.82 (.96)	-.99 (.62)	-.75 (.52)	-.24 (.25)	1.82 (.64)**
Age	-.14 (.06)*	-.07 (.04)+	-.07 (.03)*	-.01 (.02)	-.07 (.04)+
Health	-.67 (.44)	-.29 (.28)	-.22 (.24)	-.07 (.12)	-.38 (.29)
Income[b]	6.54 (3.31)*	2.77 (2.13)	1.46 (1.79)	1.28 (8.75)	3.82 (2.21)+
History of Help	.29 (.15)+	.27 (.10)**	.21 (.08)**	.06 (.04)	.02 (.10)
Race[c]	.54 (1.08)	-.43 (.69)	-.63 (.58)	.21 (.29)	.97 (.72)
Employment[d]	-.23 (1.17)	1.04 (.75)	1.25 (.63)*	-.22 (.31)	-1.27 (.78)
Constant	12.64** (4.74)	7.19* (3.05)	6.56** (2.57)	.63 (1.25)	5.47+ (3.16)
R^2	.31*** (4.05)	.40*** (2.60)	.39*** (2.19)	.22** (1.07)	.18* (2.70)

Notes: Unstandardized beta coefficients (ß). Symbols indicate significance levels: +$\leq$.10; *$\leq$.05; **$\leq$.01; ***$\leq$.001. Controlling for living parents, parents-in-law, and adult children. Standard errors in parentheses. N=106. [a] Widowed=1; married=0. [b] Family income in dollars, x 10,000. [c] White=1; black=0. [d] Employed: yes=1; no=0.

living parents, parent-in-laws or adult children, since these, in particular, may affect the "demand" for care from widows and wives.

These variables explain a significant portion of the variance (18 to 40 percent) in the number of people older widows and wives help. More importantly, when these controls are introduced, marriage drops out as a predictor of helping a greater number of recipients, with one exception. That is in the case of friends. Women who are no longer married help significantly more friends than do married women. While age and income also affect care given to friends, these effects are not nearly so significant as that of marriage. In terms of the wider community, then, being married is not a resource for informal care; widowhood is.

Hours of Care

Since marriage transforms the number of relatives and friends to whom older women give care, we might expect that it also affects the amount of *time* women spend providing that care. What we find are important differences, as well as important similarities, in the amount of time older married and widowed women spend helping family and friends.

Both widows and wives spend a great deal of time helping others. In fact, both spend the equivalent of an extra paid work week a month giving informal (and unpaid) help to family and friends (approximately 36 hours for widows and 59 hours for wives, $p \leq .05$). Also, for both, much of that time is spent caring for adult children (approximately 17 hours for widows and 33 hours for wives, $p \leq .05$).

There are important differences, however, between married and widowed women in the hours spent helping others. While both spend a remarkable amount of time helping family and friends, wives spend significantly more total hours per month in helping others than do widows (59 hours versus 36 hours, $p \leq .05$). Across specific types of kin, married women also spend significantly more time than widowed women giving care. Older married women spend more than twice as many hours as widows helping relatives overall (52 versus 25, $p \leq .01$), significantly more time helping parents (4 hours versus about 15 minutes, $p \leq .05$), nearly four times as much time helping parents-in-law (.44 versus .10 hours, $p \leq .10$) and almost twice as many hours helping adult children (33 versus 17 hours, $p \leq .05$).[1]

In contrast, widows spend significantly *more* hours than wives helping friends. In fact, they spend almost twice as much time (approximately 12 hours versus 7 hours, $p \leq .10$).

These patterns of help suggest that marriage integrates women into more intensive relations of caring overall—especially with kin—while restricting the amount of time spent caring for friends. However, the significance of these differences for total hours of help and for hours helping kin decline when appropriate controls are introduced (Table 7.2). As in the previous regressions, we control not only for physical, material and temporal resources, but also for the presence of living parents, parents-in-law and adult children. As the R^2s show, these variables as a group explain between 16 and 21 percent of the variance in the number of hours older widows and wives spend helping people they know. To be sure, widowhood (even with controls) reduces the amount of time spent helping others by approximately 16 hours. However, this is not a statistically significant reduction. Instead, it is prior history of help, not marriage or the resources associated with it, that affects total hours of care.

When we examine effects of these factors on hours helping kin and hours helping friends separately, we find that marriage itself becomes important. For

Table 7.2
OLS Regression of Hours of Help on Marriage, Age, Health, Income, History of Help, Race, and Employment

	Total Hours	Hours Kin	Hours Friends
Marriage[a]	-16.08 (3.27)	-24.03 (12.78)+	7.89 (3.63)*
Age	-.04 (.87)	-.08 (.84)	.04 (.24)
Health	-4.06 (5.10)	-3.05 (5.85)	-1.03 (1.67)
Income[b]	-15.67 (54.91)	-23.66 (44.02)	7.40 (1.26)
History of Help	5.58 (2.11)**	3.86 (2.02)+	1.72 (.58)**
Race[c]	-7.50 (14.98)	-9.60 (14.3)	2.14 (4.09)
Employment[d]	-2.93 (16.25)	-4.21 (15.57)	1.32 (4.44)
Constant	22.52 (65.80)	31.50 (63.08)	-3.56 (17.99)
R^2	.22 (56.18)**	.21 (53.86)**	.16 (.07)+

Notes: Unstandardized beta coefficients (ß). Symbols indicate significance levels: $+\leq.10$; $*\leq.05$; $**\leq.01$; $***\leq.001$. Controlling for living parents, parents-in-law, and adult children. Standard errors in parentheses. N=106.
[a] Widowed=1; married=0. [b] Family income in dollars, x 10,000. [c] White=1; black=0. [d] Employed: yes=1, no=0.

hours spent helping kin, both marriage and prior history of help are significant. Women who are married spend approximately 24 more hours per month helping kin than do widows.

For hours spent helping friends, marriage is also important. However, the direction of its effect is opposite that for kin. Married women spend an average of about 8 hours per month less than widows helping friends—regardless of other resources such as health or income. Clearly marriage reduces not only the number, but also the amount of time older women spend helping friends.

Hours Caring for Relatives and Friends: Women's Words

The qualitative data help provide explanations for different patterns of care among widows and wives. During the interviews, women frequently specified the ways in which marriage shaped giving care, suggesting that husbands were both directly and indirectly involved in this process. For some, a spouse's declining physical or mental health translated into little or no help given to nonrelatives: "I haven't done anything for friends because of my husband. He's been sick since 1982. I'm very well tied up during the day. I don't drive and I don't like to leave my husband too long. I like to be home." Comments like these were not unusual: a husband both removed a previous resource available to his wife—he used to provide transportation—and actively restrained her helping others because of his increasing need for care.

At the same time, having a husband also increases women's household labor—especially for women whose husbands do not participate in housework (far from unusual)—leaving wives weary, with little left for relationships with friends. As one 73 year-old woman explained, "Lately, I haven't had much time to do for friends. I do like to get out, but I'm not as active as some people, and I've always had someone around here, and never had much cooperation with the housework." For this woman, her husband's lack of participation in housework limits the amount of care she currently provides to friends, just as child care and primary responsibility for housework limited the amount of care she gave friends in the past.

In some cases, husbands explicitly direct their wives to limit the care they provide for nonrelatives. In discussing barriers to her giving care, one 62 year-old woman described her husband's response to her helping friends, "Sometimes he tells me I should say no for different things because I get so tired. [He'll say], 'You shouldn't have done this; you shouldn't have done that.' That's the reason I said he thinks that I do too much for friends." While this woman was involved in helping both relatives and friends, it was her helping friends to which her husband objected. In fact, during his own interview, this husband made it plain that "family comes first." His strong feelings regarding the normativeness of family care was his justification for limiting his wife's involvement in helping friends.

Some husbands, then, actively limit the help their wives give friends. They seem to legitimize that constraint by framing their objections in terms of *her* need to cut back on expenditures of energy for others. Whatever the form, explicit or implicit, legitimized or not, husbands' needs and demands took precedence. These wives' discussions of their husbands, then, help us explain why it is marriage, not widowhood, that constrains help given to friends.

Types of Care

Since marriage affects both the number of persons and amount of time women devote to caring for relatives and friends, perhaps it also affects the specific *types* of help and support women give to relatives and friends. We examine this question in two ways: first, by assessing whether or not widows and wives perform different types of tasks; second, by comparing the total number of people to whom widows and wives give each type of help.

At the most general level, married women are more likely to provide someone practical support than are widows. Married women give 3.3 types of practical help per month (doing laundry, making a meal, or repairing something, for example), compared with 2.3 types of practical help for widows ($p \leq .01$).[2] Married women are also more likely to provide personal support to at least one person than are widows—giving an average of 1.1 types of personal support per month, compared with 0.84 type of personal support for widows ($p \leq .01$).[3] However, there is no significant difference between married women and widows in whether or not they give any material help and support (e.g., give or lend money or goods). Both give slightly more than one type of material help per month (1.1 kinds of help for widows versus 1.3 types for wives).[4]

The picture is essentially the same with regard to the total number of people to whom married and widowed women provide each type of help. Married women give practical support significantly more often than do widows (7.86 versus 4.31 tasks, $p \leq .01$), as well as significantly more personal support (4.34 versus 2.23 tasks, $p \leq .01$) and more material support (4.07 versus 2.26 tasks, $p \leq .05$). Overall, then, women who are married provide more types of support, and more types of support to more people, than do widows.

A very different picture emerges when we control for the effects of other social characteristics using regression analysis. As Table 7.3 shows, marriage drops out as a significant predictor of *any* category of help and support—whether practical, personal or material. Instead of marriage, we find that age, history of help and employment each significantly affect the amount of practical support older women provide. Women who are younger, who have a greater

Table 7.3
OLS Regression of Types of Help on Marriage, Age, Health,
Income, History of Help, Race, and Employment

	Practical Help	Personal Help	Material Help
Marriage[a]	-1.58 (1.39)	-.39 (.73)	-.07 (.84)
Age	-.16 (.09)+	-.11 (.05)*	-.03 (.06)
Health	-.53 (.64)	-.07 (.34)	-.04 (.39)
Income[b]	.36 (4.81)	4.25 (2.53)+	10.88 (2.91)***
History of Help	.37 (.22)+	.17 (.12)	.09 (.13)
Race[c]	1.14 (1.57)	.48 (.83)	.83 (.95)
Employment[d]	3.63 (1.70)*	1.33 (.90)	1.06 (1.03)
Constant	12.18 (6.88)+	7.62 (3.60)*	1.87 (4.17)
R^2	.38 (5.88)***	.35 (3.09)***	.37 (3.56)***

Notes: Unstandardized beta coefficients (ß). Symbols indicate significance levels: +≤.10; *≤.05; **≤.01; ***≤.001. Controlling for having living parents, parents-in-law, and adult children. Standard errors in parentheses. N=106. [a] Widowed=1; married=0. [b] Family income in dollars, x 10,000. [c] White=1; black=0. [d] Employed: yes=1, no=0.

history of help, and who are employed give more practical support overall than do their counterparts.

Marriage also drops out as a predictor of the amount of personal support older women give people they know. Instead, we find that age and income significantly affect giving personal support—and these in opposite directions. Women who are older give less personal support, while women with greater income provide *more* personal support than do their younger or poorer counterparts.

Finally, looking at material help we find that income—not marriage—significantly affects the amount of material help older women provide. Not surprisingly, women with higher income give more material help—whether money, goods or gifts—than do older women with lower income.

Overall, we find that marriage does not significantly affect the types of help older women provide when controls are introduced for other social characteristics. Rather than marriage, we find women's age, income, history of help, and employment are significant predictors of the practical, personal and material help older women give—explaining between 35 and 38 percent of the variance in the types of tasks provided.

Types of Care: Women's Words

In many cases, women offered explanations for the types of care they provided. Older women in particular, would offer a simple "I don't drive." Or, "My children are all grown up; they don't need me to babysit now, but I used to." These types of help and support may be related to other cohort differences. Women who are older are women who reached young adulthood before transportation by automobile became commonplace; women who lived most, in some cases all, of their lives in neighborhoods where public transportation was sufficient to get them where they needed to go; women who depended on husbands and now depend on family and friends for "rides."

In general, the picture that begins to emerge is one in which both the characteristics of those to whom care is given, as well as those of the caregiver, significantly affect the types of care older married and widowed women provide. Before examining how the characteristics of the recipients affect the help older women provide (the topic of Chapter 8), I specify the distribution of these tasks among family, friends and neighbors.

The Range of Care

Finally, we detail the breadth and distribution of help to relatives and friends. In terms of total tasks, married women provide a significantly wider range of help (total number of different kinds of tasks) for every category of recipients, except friends. Overall, married women give an average of about 15 different types of help, compared with 9 types of help for widows ($p \leq .01$). The differences are even greater for the range of tasks for particular types of kin. Married women provide more than twice the range of tasks for kin that widows do (12 versus 5, $p \leq .001$). This is true whether we are considering all kin combined or own kin and in-laws separately. Married women also provide approximately twice the range of tasks for adult children as do widows (7.2 versus 3.3 tasks, $p \leq .001$), for both daughters (4.20 versus 1.82, $p \leq .01$) and sons (3.02 versus 1.55, $p \leq .01$).[5]

Although married women provide a wider range of help and support overall, and across types of kin, marriage makes no difference in the range of help older women provide to friends. In fact, widowed women provide a slightly, though not significantly, wider range of tasks for friends than married women (3.77 versus 3.11 tasks).

When controls are introduced for other social characteristics, however, marriage drops out as a significant predictor of the range of tasks older widows and wives do for family, but not friends (Table 7.4). Regardless of marriage, women who are younger, women with greater income, and women with a more extensive history of help provide a significantly wider range of help and support overall than do their counterparts. The same is true for the range of help to kin.

For particular types of kin, we find that regardless of marriage, younger women and women with a greater history of help provide a wider range of tasks for their own kin than do their counterparts. Younger women also provide a wider range of tasks for adult children—both daughters and sons—but only at the $p \leq .10$ level of significance. Looking at in-laws, we find only income is significant: Women with greater financial resources give a wider range of help to in-laws than older women with fewer financial resources. It appears, then, that the causes of care to own kin and in-laws are quite different. Financial resources are not significant in explaining care to older women's own kin, or to adult daughters and sons. However, financial resources *are* important in explaining older women's helping kin overall, and in-laws in particular, suggesting that help that is most obligatory, that to one's adult children, is less dependent on financial resources than is help that is less obligatory, such as that to in-laws.

Finally, although marriage drops out as a predictor of the range of tasks older women do for people they know overall, and for particular types of kin, this is not the case for friends. Instead, marriage significantly *decreases* the range of help women give friends. Even with controls for other social characteristics, widows provide a significantly wider range of help and support to friends than do their still married counterparts. Indeed, the only other social characteristics that matter with regard to friends are age and income—and the effects of these are less significant than that of marriage.

SUMMARY AND DISCUSSION

In summary, a number of general points should be emphasized. First, older women are significantly engaged in helping relations with family and friends. Over 90 percent of both widows and wives are involved in providing some sort of help to someone they know. Moreover, regardless of other "enabling" social characteristics such as health or income, older women spend the equivalent of an

Table 7.4
OLS Regression of Range of Tasks Given on Marriage, Age, Health, History of Help, Race, and Employment

	Total	Kin	Own Kin	Daughter	Sons	In-Laws	Friends
Marriage[a]	.12 (1.93)	-2.37 (1.46)	-1.92 (1.26)	.39 (.90)	-.31 (.70)	-.95 (.54)	2.49 (.93)**
Age	-.37 (.13)**	-.24 (.10)**	-.24 (.08)**	-.15 (.06)+	-.08 (.05)+	-.01 (.04)	-.13 (.06)+
Health	-1.22 (.89)	-.70 (.67)	.67 (.58)	.24 (.42)	-.18 (.32)	-.04 (.25)	-.52 (.43)
Income[b]	14.76 (6.67)*	8.55 (5.05)+	2.74 (4.34)	3.81 (3.12)	.27 (2.41)	4.81 (1.88)**	6.22 (3.21)+
History of Help	.88 (.31)**	.71 (.23)**	.59 (.20)**	.23 (.14)	.11 (.11)	.12 (.09)	.17 (.15)
Race[c]	.66 (2.18)	-.67 (1.65)	-.90 (1.42)	-.87 (1.02)	.23 (.79)	.23 (.61)	1.33 (1.05)
Employment[d]	2.70 (2.36)	4.03 (1.79)*	5.80 (1.54)**	1.36 (1.10)	2.77 (.85)**	-.97 (.66)	-1.33 (1.14)
Constant	28.04 (9.57)	19.18 (7.23)**	19.18 (6.22)**	10.36 (4.47)*	5.73 (3.45)+	.01 (2.68)	8.87 (4.60)
R^2	.48 (8.17)***	.53 (6.18)***	.53 (5.31)***	.33 (3.82)***	.31 (2.95)***	.32 (2.30)***	.22 (3.93)**

Notes: Unstandardized beta coefficients (ß). Symbols indicate significance levels: $+ \leq .10$; $* \leq .05$; $** \leq .01$; $*** \leq .001$. Controlling for living parents, parents-in-law, and adult children. Standard errors in parentheses. Range of tasks is the total number of tasks across 18 task types. N=106. [a] Widowed=1; married=0. [b] Family income in dollars, x 10,000. [c] White=1; black=0. [d] Employed: yes=1; no=0.

extra "work week" a month helping others. Thus, rather than being isolated or alone, the large majority of older women are engaged in actual helping behaviors with family and friends.

Second, comparing older widowed and married women, we find married women do spend significantly more hours, providing more types of care, to a larger number of kin than do widows. Most of these differences disappear, however, when controlling for other factors—especially age, income, and history of help. In fact, when other social characteristics are controlled for; it is only for hours of care to kin in general that marriage remains a significant predictor of greater help. Married women do not help a greater *number* of kin—be they their own kin or in-laws—nor do they provide significantly more of any type of help (whether practical, personal or material) or a wider range of tasks for kin than do widows, when we control for other factors.

Instead, regardless of whether or not they are married, women who are younger or more affluent provide kin *more types* of help and support than their older or poorer counterparts. Women with greater financial resources also provide more types of help and support to kin—especially money, goods and gifts—than do women with fewer financial resources. And women who have been heavily involved in helping others in the past spend more time, providing a wider range of help and support, to more kin—particularly to their own kin—than do women who have not had such a history of help.

In sharp contrast are the effects of marriage on older women's helping friends. Even with controls for other factors affecting care, women who are widowed spend significantly more hours, providing a wider range of help and support, to a larger number of friends than do married women.

There are both theoretical and practical implications of these findings. First, women's help cannot be analyzed separately from other factors which affect their ability to provide care. In particular, scholars who argue that marriage is an integrating institution overstate the case. The kinkeeping responsibilities that women take on with marriage (or the marriages of their children) persist after the loss of a spouse. However, while marriage may integrate older women into relations of caring for kin, this is clearly not the case for friends and neighbors. The help older women give friends is an altogether different matter. While widows may have fewer material and physical resources available for giving care, what they *do* have are more time and more freedom. It is these resources that widowed women channel into helping friends. While some have argued that friends are good for marriage (Oliker, 1989; Rubin, 1985), these data suggest that marriage is not particularly good for friends. Instead, it privatizes women's care—providing them with resources and opportunity to help kin, while isolating them, at least in relative terms, from those outside the family.

These findings have implications for theories of aging which stress shrinking social networks and gradual disengagement as part of the aging process. While the number of relations to whom care is given may decline with age, the amount of time spent in helping others does not. That is, intensive relations of caring may replace extensive community ties. So, too, in emphasizing gradual withdrawal from broader social relations "into" the family, theories of disengagement gloss over important and subtle differences between married women and widows. Rather than simply disengaging from caring relations as they grow older, women reorganize their caring at each life transition. As we have seen, helping kin in general does not appear to be affected by the loss of the "wife role." Women who are caregivers—those with a long history of providing help and support to kin—and those with continuing material or financial resources are active in providing help and support to kin regardless of whether they are currently married or widowed.

The loss of the "wife role" does, however, affect helping nonkin, independent of age. In fact, the absence of a spouse is associated with an expansion of women's helping friends. In this sense, widowed women may experience a "role gain" at the same time as they experience a "role loss" after their husband's death. Thus, widows reengage with friends at a time when they may also disengage from some of their caring relations with kin.

NOTES

1. Women who had, but did not help, parents, parent-in-laws, or adult children, and women without parents, parent-in-laws, or adult children were both treated as having spent zero hours helping those relations. This was done for both methodological and conceptual reasons. First, omitting respondents who did not have parents, parents-in-law, or adult children would severely limit the number of cases available for analysis (since when one or the other of these relations was missing, the entire case would be dropped from the analysis). Second, those who do not have these relatives do not experience the same "demands" for care that parents, parents-in-laws or adult children represent.

It is worth noting that when hours of help are compared for only those widows and wives who have parents, parents-in-law and adult children, the pattern of significant differences between widows and wives remains the same as when those without these relations are omitted. Married women who have living parents, parents-in-law, and adult children spend significantly more hours than their widowed counterparts helping parents (28 hours versus 7 hours, p=.07), parents-in-law (6 hours versus 1 hour, p=.03), and adult children (38 hours versus 20 hours, p=.05).

2. At the level of individual practical tasks, married women are significantly more likely than widows to do laundry (46 versus 28 percent, p≤.05), repair something (38 versus 16 percent, p≤.01), give a ride (55 versus 37 percent, p≤.05), provide child care (49 versus 26 percent, p≤.01), or care for someone

who is sick (38 versus 24 percent, p≤.05).

3. At the level of individual tasks, wives are significantly more likely than widows to give personal help in the form of talk about personal problems or concerns (84 versus 59 percent, p≤.01) and giving advice about employment (11 percent versus 4 percent, p≤.10).

4. At the level of individual tasks, widowed women are as likely as wives to give money (63 versus 80 percent), goods (20 versus 24 percent), or gifts (57 versus 64 percent).

5. Older women without adult daughters or sons were assigned a zero for the range of tasks performed for adult children. When the range of tasks for widows and wives is compared only for women who have adult children, the results are essentially the same. Married women with adult children, whether daughters or sons, provide approximately twice the range of tasks for their adult children that widows do.

8

Marriage and the Recipients of Care

INTRODUCTION

The relationship of the person receiving care clearly makes a difference in whether marriage is greedy and restricts giving care, or integrative and increases it. But marriage may be greedy, or integrative, not only as an institution that takes priority over other relations. Marriage involves another person—a spouse. The greediness of marriage, then, may also lie in the "greediness" of husbands who manage wives' use of energy, money, and time. Husbands may control family finances. They may encourage some activities (and discourage others) and establish the parameters of time wives can spend helping others by requiring meals or company at certain times of day.

Although we do not have data on how husbands directly shape wives' help to family and friends, we may infer some of these influences by examining the links between the characteristics of the recipients and the kinds of help married and widowed women provide.

BACKGROUND

Scattered research suggests that both the relative need of the recipient (lower income or poorer health, for example) and the homogeneity of gender and marital status may be important in shaping what and to whom older women give care. Most of this research focuses on help given to adult children and to friends.

Recipients of Care: Adult Children

Recent work on intergenerational relations provides several relevant findings regarding the ways in which adult children's characteristics affect the help older married and widowed women provide (Rossi and Rossi, 1990). Geographic proximity and children's income similarly affect help provided by both widowed and still married mothers. Adult children who live closer or whose income is lower, receive more help than their more distant or better-off counterparts. The gender of an adult child also affects the amount of help they receive. But this seems to matter more for widows than for wives. Older women, especially those who are still married, give more support to daughters than to sons. Older women also give more help to single and divorced daughters than to those who are married. But, again, this is true more of married women than of widows. Whether sons are married or not has no effect on the help they receive, regardless of their mother's marital status.

Two points are apparent from Rossi and Rossi's work. First, children's gender and marital status are important in shaping the help they receive from aging mothers. Second, these effects seem to be greater for married women than for widows—suggesting that marriage both integrates women into helping relations and enables them to be particularly responsive to adult children who are themselves not married and may have greater need for care.

Recipients of Care: Friends and Neighbors

Older women's help to friends and neighbors may also be affected by the characteristics of those they help. Earlier work on friendship suggests widows' interaction with friends is affected more by geographic proximity than is wives' (Hochschild, 1973; Rosow, 1967; Townsend, 1957). To the extent that caring takes place within the context of interaction, we might expect to find a similar pattern for help provided. Whether friends are similarly married or unmarried may also affect the help they receive. Widowed women tend to interact more with women who are themselves no longer married, while wives tend to interact more with women who are married (Lopata, 1973; Rosow, 1967; Townsend, 1957).

HYPOTHESES

This chapter tests several hypotheses about the ways in which the help older widows and wives give friends is linked to the characteristics of those receiving care. In general, previous research suggests that the effects of recipient characteristics on giving care may be different for widows and wives. At the same time, these effects may vary depending on whether we are considering help to adult children or help to friends and neighbors. These also may vary depending on whether we are considering characteristics that indicate the recipient's need or characteristics that facilitate giving care. These three considerations—the marital status of the giver, the type of relation, and the relative ease or difficulty of giving care—produce a set of complicated and somewhat contradictory expectations for the effects of recipients' characteristics on help received.

Looking, first, at recipient's gender: to the extent that giving care follows patterns of interaction, we might expect both widows and wives to help other women more than men. However, the gender of the recipient may affect married women's giving help more than that of widows—especially in the case of adult children. This is for two reasons. First, married women have greater material resources to be used in helping others. Daughters, on the other hand, may have greater needs for care since they typically earn less than men and bear more responsibility for domestic work and child care. This would be especially true for daughters who are unmarried. Both married and widowed women may feel similarly obligated to help adult daughters more than sons. However, because married women's resources may make the help they provide more elastic or responsive to the needs of those they help, we may find that the gender of an adult child has greater effect on care given by wives than on care given by widows. To the extent, then, that gender captures relative need, we might expect to find no difference in the help widows provide sons and daughters, while wives provide significantly more help to daughters than to sons.

Friends' gender, however, may have less of an effect on the help older widows and wives provide. Having a husband links married women into relations in which wives help their husbands' friends (Chappell, 1983; Fischer and Oliker, 1983)—relations perhaps less available to widows. While married women may use their greater resources to help female friends, married women may also be obligated, through their husbands, to help male friends as well. If these effects cancel each other out, friends' gender may show little significant net effect on the help wives give friends.

In contrast, while widows lack both the financial and the social resources marriage provides, the findings in Chapter 5 suggest widowed women may have greater control than wives over how these resources are used in helping others. As a result, widows may give *more* help than wives to family and friends who are female, and to those who have greater needs for care—whether through poorer health or lower income. Gender, health, and income, then, may have more significant effects on the help widows provide than on that given by wives.

Previous research also suggests competing hypotheses about the effects of recipient's marriage on the help older women provide. On the one hand, to the extent that giving help follows obligations to help, we might expect adult children who are not married to receive more help than children who are married, especially from married women who have more resources (money, if not time) to give. On the other hand, to the extent that helping others follows patterns of interaction, marriage among recipients may have very different effects on the help widows and wives provide—especially in the case of friends and neighbors. Married women may help *married* friends, and widowed women more unmarried friends, on the basis of similarity of marital status. When degree of need (recipients' income) and caregiver's material resources are controlled for, we might expect the marital status of the recipient to be positively associated with help from older married women, and negatively associated with help from women who are widowed.

ANALYSIS

We begin by examining differences in widows' and wives' help to different types of kin, looking specifically at the ways in which helping kin varies depending on the gender of the recipient. Then we assess the effects of marriage on the types of help older women give to adult children and friends. As in Chapter 5, regression analysis is used to separate the effects of recipients' marriage, gender, and income on the amount of practical, personal and material support provided. In addition, we assess the effects of characteristics facilitating giving care: recipients' geographic proximity, affective closeness and marital status (either married or unmarried). In the case of adult children, equations are run separately for help to daughters and sons. In the case of friends, the gender of the recipient is included in the equation as an independent variable. In both cases, the unit of analysis is the individual helped. Key characteristics of the older women giving help (self-reported physical health, age and income) are repeated and matched with data for each individual helped.

Widows and Wives Helping Male and Female Kin

Table 8.1 shows the probability of married and widowed women helping a number of different types of male and female relatives: parents, adult children, siblings, in-laws, and grandchildren. What is immediately clear is that the gender of the recipient makes a difference in whether or not older women provide care—especially with regard to adult children and siblings (though not, to the same degree, other relatives). More specifically, married women are more likely than widows to provide help and support to daughters, but not sons. Married women are also more likely than widows to help sisters (but not brothers), and brothers-in-law (but not sisters-in-law). Married women are *not*, however, more likely than widows to help mothers, fathers, sons, brothers, mothers-in-law, fathers-in-law, daughters-in-law, sons-in-law, sisters-in-law, or grandchildren (either granddaughters or grandsons).

Table 8.1
Married and Widowed Women's Help to Different Recipients

I. Help given to	% Who Helped		Number Helped	
	Married	Widowed	Married	Widowed
Parents[a]	.13	.04+	.13	.04+
Mother	.07	.04	--	--
Father	.05	.00	--	--
Adult Children[a]	.76	.63+	2.31	1.24**
Daughter	.64	.43*	1.27	.67**
Son	.53	.45	1.04	.57*
Siblings	.35	.18*	.65	.22**
Sister	.29	.12**	.49	.12**
Brother	.11	.08	.16	.10
In-Laws[a]	.07	.04	.07	.04
Mother-in-Law	.07	.04	--	--
Father-in-Law	.00	.00	--	--
Daughter/Son in-Law	.11	.08	.16	.08
Daughter-in-Law	.11	.06	.15	.06
Son-in-Law	.02	.02	.02	.02
Brother/Sister in-Law	.29	.18+	.47	.20+
Sister-in-Law	.22	.16	.31	.16+
Brother-in-Law	.15	.04*	.16	.04*
Grandchild	.20	.26	.44	.35

Notes: Symbols indicate level of significance: +≤.10; *≤.05; **≤.01; ***≤.001.
Married, N=55; widowed, N=51. [a] Those who do not have this relation, and
those who have but do not help, are both coded as 0.

A similar pattern is evident for the number of each type of relative helped. Not surprisingly, given their younger age, married women help more parents than do older widows—younger women have more parents alive to be helped. Married women also help a greater number of adult children (both daughters and sons), sisters (but not brothers), and sisters-in-law and brothers-in-law than do widows. Widows, on the other hand, do not help significantly more of any type of kin, although they do help as many brothers, as many parents-in-law, as many daughters-in-law and sons-in-law, and as many grandsons and granddaughters as do married women.

Importantly, where there are significant differences between widows and wives is in helping other women relatives—with two exceptions: sons and brothers-in-law. Married women help more sons and more brothers-in-law than do widows. We examine help to sons and daughters more specifically later. But why do wives help more brothers-in-law than do women who are no longer married? One possible explanation is that married women's help to sisters spills over to brothers-in-law: sisters are helped, and so too are brothers-in-law. It may also be that the husbands of still married women provide a link through which help is given to brothers-in-law—a link no longer available to women who are widowed. Whatever the actual process, wives' help to brothers-in-law illustrates the power of marriage to expand helping kin.

In most cases, where marriage makes a difference in older women's help to kin, we find married women helping more kin—especially more female kin—than do widows. Looking at this from a different angle, we can compare help within pairs of male and female relatives. Gender makes little difference in widowed women's help to kin. Widows help similar numbers of male and female kin, except in the case of helping more sisters-in-laws than brothers-in-law. In contrast, married women help significantly more female kin across each kin type. It is only in helping adult children that we find no significant difference between the number of daughters and sons helped. Both widowed and married women help similar numbers of sons and daughters.

Overall, then, while married women help more kin than do widows, this is especially true for female kin. It may be that older women's help to female kin declines more rapidly after widowhood than does help to male kin. In several instances, widows suggested their own explanations as they discussed the help they give siblings. One widow, explaining how she and seven sisters shared the burden of caring for their mother, said, "I help my brother with his housekeeping. He used to live with my mother until she went into the nursing home. He's a bachelor; now I'm supposed to help him clean *his* house." This brother received routine help from his sister while he was living with their elderly mother. Although she resisted, it is extraordinary that this woman continued to do routine cleaning for her brother even after their mother was moved into a nursing home. In contrast, widows described sisters, themselves likely to be caregivers, as being less "in need" of care. Sisters were more "independent"; or, when they did give help, widows linked that care to peculiar needs, rather than routine care. As one woman explained:

> My sister died last October. I used to go over and give her insulin and clean for her for 2 years. I did all her shopping. She wore me out. I used to go back and forth five or six times a day. I think that's why I'm sick now: she wore me out. My youngest sister just lost her daughter in April. She confides in me a lot. We go to the cemetery and spend Sundays together.

It may be, as these widows' comments suggest, that help to sisters is more linked to specific needs, while help to brothers is more routine. It is to the effects of relative need on the help widows and wives give that we now turn.

Widow's and Wive's Help to Adult Children

Because data were collected on adult children regardless of whether or not they were helped, it is possible to examine the ways in which adult children's characteristics variously affect help received. Table 8.2 shows the likelihood of widows' and wives' providing practical, personal and material support to adult sons and daughters. Widowed women are as likely as married women to give practical help to adult children—sons, but not daughters. Widows are *less* likely than wives to give practical help to daughters. They are also less likely than wives to give either personal or material help to either sons or daughters.

The picture with regard to the number of tasks performed for daughters and sons is only slightly different. Across types of support and gender of adult child, married women perform a greater *number* of tasks than widows. At the level of individual tasks, married women give more personal support in the form of talking about problems or concerns, and more material support in the form of giving more gifts to both daughters and sons. Married women also give more practical support in the form of repairs and child care to both daughters and sons, and do more laundry and give more rides for sons (but not daughters) than do widows. Widows, on the other hand, give daughters and sons as much help with meals, care when sick, cleaning, advice, money and goods as married women.

Overall, then, married women give more of each type of help to adult children than do widows. But does the gender of the adult child affect help received from widowed mothers differently than help received from mothers who are still married? Stated differently, do widows allocate help to adult daughters and sons differently than do wives? Looking at Table 8.2 again, we can compare type of help to paired daughters and sons. Both widowed and married women

Table 8.2
Tasks Married Women and Widows Do for Adult Children

Type of Help[a]	Yes/No		Number	
	Married	Widowed	Married	Widowed
I. Practical Help	.73	.64	4.19	2.31**
	(.45)	(.49)	(3.81)	(2.65)
Daughters	.71	.54+	2.88	1.93+
	(.46)	(.51)	(2.94)	(2.58)
Sons	.58	.60	2.18	1.23*
	(.58)	(.50)	(2.43)	(1.40)
II. Personal Help	.77	.43***	2.17	.95***
	(.43)	(.50)	(2.09)	(1.27)
Daughters	.71	.50*	1.39	.79*
	(.46)	(.51)	(1.41)	(1.00)
Sons	.63	.31**	1.24	.51**
	(.46)	(.51)	(1.30)	(.85)
III. Material Help	.60	.33**	1.83	.76**
	(.49)	(.48)	(2.14)	(1.25)
Daughters	.61	.32**	1.29	.54**
	(.49)	(.48)	(1.57)	(.88)
Sons	.45	.23*	.92	.49*
	(.50)	(.43)	(1.24)	(1.04)

Notes: Symbols indicate level of significance for a one-tailed test of difference between means for married and widowed women, using a separate estimate of variance: $+\leq.10$; $*\leq.05$; $**\leq.01$; $***\leq.001$. Widows, N=51; Wives, N=55. Standard deviations in parentheses. Those who do not have adult children, daughters or sons, and those who have but do not help, are both coded as missing. [a] Mean number of practical, personal and material tasks done for adult daughters and sons in the previous month.

give slightly more of each type of help to daughters than to sons. However, none of these differences reaches statistical significance. This contradicts the hypothesis that married women, more than widows, give more help to daughters than to sons.

Effects of Children's Characteristics on Help Received. Table 8.3 shows the results of a regression analysis for widows' and wives' practical, personal and material help to adult daughters and sons. The independent variables included are of three types: characteristics of the *recipients* that facilitate giving care (geographic proximity and emotional closeness), relative need for care (health, income, and marriage), and characteristics of the *caregivers* that reflect their material, physical and temporal resources available for helping others (their income, health, and employment).[1]

Together these variables explain between 33 and 45 percent of the variance in the number of practical, personal and material tasks older widows and wives do for adult daughters and son. The significance of individual variables, however, varies considerably for the help widows and wives provide. In particular, children's income, health, and marriage significantly affect the help widows give more frequently than wives across types of help and gender of adult child. Widows give more practical and more material help to daughters who are in poor health, while wives give only more material help. Widows also give more of each type of help—whether practical, personal, or material—to sons who are not married, while the help older married women give sons is unaffected by whether or not sons are married. Interestingly, help from widows and wives is more similarly affected by whether or not daughters are married. Older married women give more personal support to daughters who are married than to daughters who are unmarried, while widowed mothers give married daughters more material support than their unmarried counterparts. It appears, then, that women without husbands help sons without wives, while daughters *with* husbands get help from both widows and wives.

Like children's marriage, children's income also affects help from widowed mothers more than help from mothers who are still married. Widows give more of each type of help to children who are poor—both daughters and sons—than to children who are better off financially. In contrast, wives help poorer daughters and sons with more personal support, but not more material or practical support. Thus, children in financial need receive only more comfort and advice from mothers who are married, while adult children in financial need receive more comfort and advice, as well as more practical and material help and support, from mothers who are widowed.

Finally, characteristics that facilitate giving care—adult children's geographic proximity and affective closeness—have relatively similar effects on help received from both widowed and married mothers. Greater affective closeness increases widows' practical help to daughters, as well as wives' personal help to

Table 8.3
OLS Regression of Types of Help Widows and Wives Give Adult Children on Respondent and Recipient Characteristics

A. Widows	Practical Help		Personal Help		Material Help	
<u>Respondent Characteristics</u>	Daughter	Son	Daughter	Son	Daughter	Son
Employment	-.09 (.61)	.05 (.37)	-.15 (.23)	.35 (.24)	-.00 (.23)	.30 (.28)
Health	-.41 (.22)+	-.30 (.17)+	.12 (.08)	-.14 (.11)	-.03 (.08)	-.17 (.13)
Income	2.24 (2.69)	-.12 (1.96)	3.11 (1.03)**	-.52 (1.28)	.85 (1.00)	-2.06 (1.47)
<u>Recipient Characteristics</u> Geographic Proximity	-.17 (.11)	-.34 (.09)***	.09 (.04)*	.01 (.06)	-.07 (.04)+	.08 (.07)
Health	.68 (.33)*	.10 (.17)	-.10 (.13)	.11 (.11)	.24 (.12)+	.12 (.13)
Income	-.62 (.28)*	-.37 (.19)+	-.27 (.11)*	-.36 (.13)**	-.41(.11)***	-.46 (.14)**
Closeness	.65 (.29)*	.33 (.17)*	-.00 (.11)	.17 (.11)	.06 (.11)	.01 (.12)
Marriage	-.31 (.44)	-.70 (.26)**	.05 (.17)	-.47 (.17)**	.28 (.16)+	-.50 (.20)**
R²	.43 (1.21)**	.45 (.83)***	.40 (.46)**	.37 (.54)**	.43 (.45)**	.33 (.62)**

Notes: Unstandardized beta coefficients (ß). Significance levels: +≤.10; *≤.05; **≤.01; ***≤.001. Standard error in parentheses. Widows have sons, N=56; daughters, N=49. See Notes, Table 5.2, for a description of these variables.

114

B. Wives

Respondent Characteristics	Practical Help		Personal Help		Material Help	
	Daughter	Son	Daughter	Son	Daughter	Son
Employment[a]	-.38 (.34)	-.26 (.38)	.33 (.13)*	-.11 (.16)	-.01 (.19)	.17 (.18)
Health	-.42 (.23)+	-.41 (.21)+	-.13 (.09)	-.18 (.09)*	-.05 (.13)	-.13 (.10)
Income[b]	-.01 (1.01)	-.19 (1.23)	.73 (.40)+	.16 (.49)	2.39 (.56)***	.75 (.56)
Recipient Characteristics						
Geographic Proximity	-.52 (.08)***	-.25 (.10)*	-.06(.03)+	.01 (.04)	-.14 (.05)**	-.02 (.05)
Health	.16 (.24)	.11 (.25)	.04 (.10)	.09 (.11)	.31 (.14)*	.19 (.12)
Income	-.17 (.24)	-.08 (.27)	-.25 (.10)**	-.25 (.12)*	-.19 (.14)	.07 (.14)
Closeness	.20 (.26)	.28 (.28)	-.01 (.10)	.22 (.12)+	.05 (.14)	.17 (.14)
Marriage	.04 (.35)	-.23 (.43)	.26 (.14)+	-.15 (.19)	.20 (.19)	-.08 (.21)
R²	.41 (1.29)***	.25 (1.31)*	.29 (.51)**	.24 (.57)*	.34 (.72)***	.21 (.64)+

Notes: Unstandardized beta coefficients (β). Significance levels: +≤.10; *≤.05; **≤.01; ***≤.001. Standard error in parentheses. Wives have sons, N=74; daughters, N=88. See Notes, Table 5.2, for a description of these variables.

sons.[2] Being geographically close also increases widows' and wives' help to adult children. Both widows and wives give more practical support to sons who live nearby than to sons who live farther away. Both widowed and married women also give more material help to daughters who live close than to those who live farther away. Married women, however, also give more practical as well as more personal support to daughters who live close than those farther away.

Overall, then, the help widowed women give adult children appears to be more affected by their children's needs than is help from still married mothers. Because we have seen that widows give significantly less of each type of help to adult children than do wives (see Table 8.2), this suggests widows help adult children in response to particular needs, while wives help adult children in more routine, everyday ways.

Friends' Characteristics and Help from Widows and Wives

Finally, we examine the ways in which marriage affects older women's help to friends. Table 8.4 compares the practical, personal, and material help and support widows and wives give friends and neighbors. Widows and wives are more likely to provide practical help than either personal or material support to friends. Being married does not significantly affect the percentage of women

Table 8.4
Tasks Married Women and Widows Do for Friends and Neighbors (t-Tests)

	Percent Who Give		Number of Tasks Given[a]	
Type of Help[a]	Married Women	Widowed Women	Married Women	Widowed Women
Practical Help	.44 (.50)	.59+ (.50)	1.18 (1.91)	1.65 (2.75)
Personal Help	.44 (.50)	.45 (.50)	.96 (1.69)	.88 (1.44)
Material Help	.35 (.48)	.35 (.48)	.78 (1.50)	.92 (1.87)

Notes: Symbols indicate level of significance: $+\leq.10$; $*\leq.05$; $**\leq.01$; $***\leq.001$. Standard deviations in parentheses. Widows, N=51; wives, N=55. [a] Mean number of practical, personal and material tasks done for friends in the previous month.

who give personal or material help to friends. Nor do widows and wives significantly differ in the number of different types of practical, personal or material support they give friends. Marriage does, however, slightly depress the percentage of women who give practical help to friends. Forty-four percent of the wives, compared with 59 percent of the women who are widowed, give practical help to friends.

Effects of Friends' Characteristics on Help Received. Using regression analysis, we can examine the ways in which friends' characteristics affect these types of support (Table 8.5). We have data on friends helped, as well as any friends who gave but did not receive help in the past month. Together, these represent a fairly complete list of friends. For the purposes of this analysis, we assume either (1) that the list of friends is complete (defining friends as those to whom or from whom help was given in the past month) or (2) that friends not mentioned do not significantly differ from friends included in the list. Table 8.5 shows the results of this analysis.

What is immediately apparent in Table 8.5 is that when other characteristics are controlled for, neither widows' nor wives' help to friends is affected by friend's needs—in terms of either poorer health or less income. In fact, in the one instance where income is significant, it is wealthier friends who receive more care—from married women, but not widows—rather than friends who are poor. As with wives' help to adult children, this suggests the material help married women give friends may be everyday gifts of money or goods, rather than help given to meet specific material needs among friends.

Table 8.5 also shows that none of the types of help and support married women give friends is significantly affected by whether friends are married or unmarried. In contrast, marriage does predict widowed women's helping friends, holding constant other key characteristics. Somewhat surprisingly, however, widows give more material support to friends who are married, rather than to those who are unmarried. Being similarly married or unmarried may be an important factor in older women's interaction with friends and neighbors. However, help to friends is not consistently linked to friends' marital status.

Finally, just as homogeneity of marriage does not significantly increase the help widows and wives give friends, neither does homogeneity of gender significantly affect help to friends. No type of help—whether practical, personal or material—from either widows or wives is significantly affected by friends' gender. Thus, while gender may be important in predicting interaction with friends—particularly among widowed women—gender does not affect the help widows and wives give friends and neighbors.

Table 8.5
OLS Regression of Types of Help Widows and Wives Give Friends and Neighbors on Respondent and Recipient Characteristics

	Practical Help		Personal Help		Material Help	
	Widows	Wives	Widows	Wives	Widows	Wives
Respondent Characteristics						
Employment	-.40 (.28)	-.14 (.21)	.42 (.19)*	.01 (.13)	-.11 (.19)	.28 (.10)**
Health	-.22 (.06)***	.15 (.20)	.07 (.04)+	.08 (.12)	.07 (.04)+	-.12 (.10)
Income	1.18 (.92)	-.13 (.64)	-.08 (.62)	-.16 (.39)	-.03 (.62)	.15 (.32)
Recipient Characteristics						
Geographic Proximity	-.12 (.04)**	-.05 (.08)	-.01 (.03)	-.01 (.05)	.06 (.03)*	.06 (.04)
Health	-.01 (.07)	-.12 (.10)	.00 (.05)	.06 (.06)	-.03 (.05)	-.01 (.05)
Income	.00 (.10)	-.05 (.17)	-.02 (.07)	-.15 (.10)	.06 (.07)	.23 (.09)**
Closeness	.01 (.06)	.09 (.10)	.08 (.04)*	.14 (.06)**	-.00 (.04)	-.01 (.05)
Marriage	.05 (.14)	-.19 (.20)	-.11 (.09)	-.08 (.12)	.19 (.09)*	.07 (.10)
Gender	-.02 (.14)	.07 (.25)	-.13 (.10)	.01 (.15)	.09 (.10)	.14 (.12)
R^2	.18 (.69)**	.05 (.87)	.14 (.45)*	.12 (.53)	.15 (.46)**	.28 (.44)**

Notes: Unstandardized beta coefficients (ß). Significance levels: +$\leq$.10; *$\leq$.05; **$\leq$.01; ***$\leq$.001. Standard error in parentheses. See Notes, Table 5.2, for a description of these variables. Number of friends helped by widows=144, by wives=107.

SUMMARY AND DISCUSSION

These findings largely contradict the hypothesis that homogeneity of gender and marital status significantly affects the help widowed and married women give family and friends. The gender of the recipient has no effect on the kinds of help either widows or wives give people they know. Although being similarly female may be important in shaping patterns of interaction with family and friends, this is not the case for patterns of help and support. The effects of being similarly married or unmarried are only slightly more significant. Only widows' help to friends is affected by friends' marriage, and they give more material support to friends who are married, rather than unmarried.

The effects of adult children's characteristics on help received tell a different story. These more clearly reveal the importance of marriage in shaping the kinds of help married and widowed mothers give adult daughters and sons. Widowed mothers can be seen picking up the slack—and the laundry, and dishes, and toys—in daughters' homes when daughters are poorer, or in poor health and less able to cope with the practical tasks of running a household. Widowed women can also be seen giving all types of help and support to sons who are poorer, especially those who are unmarried, than to sons who are less poor. In contrast, married women may phone and visit adult daughters and sons who are in need financially, or daughters who are married—giving emotional support, listening, and giving advice, but not cooking, cleaning or performing a significant amount of the practical work that keeps a household running.

The effects of adult children's characteristics on the help older women provide also tell us something about the greediness of husbands. While the personal support wives give adult children is linked to the material and physical needs of their daughters and sons, each type of help given by widows—whether practical, personal, or material—is greater to children who have greater needs. Clearly, while widows may not have more money than wives, what they do have is more time and more say over how their money (and time) are spent—and one of things they spend it on is helping their daughters and sons. Moreover, widows specifically give more of each type of help and support to unmarried sons than to sons who are married—suggesting that some of the care previously given to husbands may be transferred to sons without wives.

Overall, then, the help widowed women give tends to be more affected by recipients' relative need than is the help older married women provide, while the characteristics of the recipients that facilitate giving care similarly affect help from both widows and wives. These trends suggest something about the character of the help widows and wives give, as well as the ways in which marriage shapes older women's help to family and friends. Because wives give more help than widows overall, and because help from widowed women is more linked to the needs of those they help than is that from wives, it would seem that a large part of the help widows give—to family in particular—consists of help given to meet specific, sometimes acute needs. In contrast, the help married women give may consist more of everyday help and support—the "nothings" that are essential to maintaining links with family and friends.

These findings also speak to the ways in which marriage inhibits women's altruism. Because the wives' help to family and friends is not significantly affected by the needs of the recipients, it is not altruistic in the same sense as is the help widows provide. Widowed mothers' help to adult children, in particular, is clearly linked to the needs of those they help, whereas help wives give is not. Still, it cannot be inferred that married women are less generous in helping others than are widows—after all, as we saw in the previous chapter, married women spend more time and help a larger number of relatives than do widows.

The picture that emerges from this analysis is one where older wives help more family on an everyday basis, but are constrained by marriage from giving help in response to specific material or physical needs in a way that widowed women are not. Widows, in contrast, may give less support to fewer people overall than do wives, yet they are freer to help those who are in need.

NOTES

1. Geographic proximity of the recipient is coded from 0=in the same household, to 6=more than 2 hours away. Emotional closeness is coded from 0=not at all close to 4=extremely close. Health of the recipient is coded from 0=excellent to 4=very poor. The relative financial status of the recipient is coded from 0=not enough to get by to 3=more than enough to get by. Recipients' marital status is included as dummy variable for married=1, not married=0. Characteristics of the *caregivers* include total family income in dollars, health (coded from 0=excellent to 4=very poor) and employment (1=employed, 0=not employed).

2. Feeling close may be a cause as well as a consequence of giving more help. However, if closeness were *just* a consequence of giving care, we might expect to find more consistency in its effects across types of care and gender of adult child. Also, if affective closeness were primarily a consequence and not a cause of greater giving care, we would expect women's closeness to adult daughters and sons to increase with the amount of personal support older women provide. However, that is not the case. When the equations are reestimated with closeness as the dependent variable, personal support is not a significant predictor of affective closeness between either married or widowed women and their daughters and sons.

9

Marriage and Giving Help
through Formal Volunteerism

Marriage privatizes women's informal help to family and friends, at the same time that it limits the types of help and support older women give others in need. We might expect the "greediness" of marriage to be evident in patterns of help to those who are neither family nor friends as well. Yet, because marriage provides social and material resources, it may also increase the help older women give nonkin through their participation in formal volunteer efforts. This chapter turns from informal help to family and friends to assess the impact of marriage on older women's volunteerism.

BACKGROUND

Previous research suggests marriage has little effect on either the number of groups helped or amount of time older women spend volunteering. Lopata (1973) argues that participation in volunteer groups generally declines after widowhood. However, because her analysis does not systematically control for health and income, it leaves open the question of whether it is loss of a husband itself, or the declining physical and material resources that accompany widowhood that causes this decline group participation. When health and income are controlled for, marriage does not significantly affect the percentage of older women who volunteer (Altergott, 1985; Chambre, 1984), especially in religious groups (Petrowsky, 1976). Nor does it significantly affect the amount of time older women spend volunteering, independent of health and income (Altergott, 1985).

Marriage may, however, influence the types of groups to which older women belong. Widows belong to different kinds of groups—typically smaller, all-female groups—than their married counterparts (McPherson and Smith-Lovin, 1986). Perhaps this is because married women are drawn into more couple oriented groups than are widows. If so, marriage may expand women's integration into the community, but have little effect on women's own commitment to volunteering.

Marriage also does not operate alone in shaping older women's participation in volunteer associations. In addition to the effects of health and income, previous research also finds that employment increases volunteer group membership (McPherson and Smith-Lovin, 1982). Although the effect of employment may be less among older women than within the general population, it also has a positive effect on the percentage of widows and wives who volunteer (Chambre, 1984).

HYPOTHESES

While somewhat limited, findings from previous research on older women's volunteerism suggest several hypotheses about the ways in which marriage affects participation, number of memberships, and the amount of time older women devote to caring for others through volunteer associations. First, just as marriage integrates women into larger networks of kin, marriage may also integrate them into a larger number of volunteer associations. If so, we would expect older married women to belong to a larger number of such associations than widows.

Second, marriage is likely to limit the amount of time women spend volunteering. Marriage may be "greedy" with regard to time spent helping others through formal volunteerism, as it is in time spent helping friends and neighbors (Chapter 7). To the extent that this is the case, we would expect married women to spend less time volunteering than widows.

Third, marriage may affect the types of groups to which older women belong. In particular, it may draw them into groups in which their husbands are active—groups to which wives otherwise may not be as likely to belong. Wives, then, may belong to more service and political groups than do widows, while widows belong to more religious or welfare groups than do wives.

Fourth, while marriage may limit older women's volunteerism, it also provides greater material resources for helping others. Married women's higher family income in particular may offset the "greediness" of marriage itself. Thus, when income is controlled for, the effects of marriage on volunteerism may decline (if not disappear). In addition, physical health, as well as employment, may also affect older women's participation in volunteer activities. We might expect poorer health to have fairly straightforward effects on volunteerism— limiting both the extent of women's involvement and their commitment to volunteering. The effects of women's employment, however, may be somewhat contradictory. Employment may draw older women into a larger number of groups—particularly job oriented groups—while reducing the time women have for volunteering. Thus, older women who are employed may belong to more groups but spend fewer hours volunteering than women who are not employed.

Finally, previous research suggests competing hypotheses about the ways in which informal help to family and friends may affect the help women give others through formal volunteer efforts. Obligations to care for kin and friends are clearly stronger than obligations to care for strangers (Rossi and Rossi, 1990). To the extent that giving help follows a similar pattern, we would expect more time helping family and friends to mean less time volunteering to help others. Helping family and friends, however, may integrate women into a larger number of volunteer associations, as older women are encouraged to volunteer by those they help. To the extent that this is the case, we would expect helping family and friends to increase, rather than decrease, older women's volunteerism.

ANALYSIS

This chapter assesses the effects of marriage on three aspects of older women's volunteer efforts: their degree of participation (whether they belong, the number of groups in which they participate, and the amount of time spent volunteering), the types of groups to which older women belong, and the kinds of work done by highly involved volunteers. Each of these captures a different dimension of helping others through volunteer associations, whether the character and breadth of women's involvement in the wider community, the depth of their commitment to volunteering, or the degree to which these activities provide avenues for helping those in need.

Women's Participation: Numbers and Hours

Table 9.1 compares the mean number of groups and mean number of hours married and widowed women devote to volunteer activities. A slightly larger percentage of married than widowed women belong to at least one volunteer group (67 versus 57 percent). Married women also belong to slightly more groups (2.12 versus 1.84) and spend slightly more hours a month in volunteer activities. However, none of these differences is statistically significant. At this most general level, it appears that marriage has little impact on older women's volunteerism.

When controls are introduced for key variables affecting the resources women draw on to help others, several important differences emerge (Table 9.2). Along with age, health, income, and employment, these equations also control for the effects of history of help, race and hours of help to family and friends.[1] As the R^2s in Table 9.2 show, together these variables are more effective in explaining the variance in the number of groups to which women belong than the

Table 9.1
Volunteerism Among Widowed and Married Women
(t-Tests)

	Married Women (mean)	Widowed Women (mean)
Any Groups (% helping)	.67 (.49)	.57 (.50)
Total Groups (mean #)	2.13 (2.19)	1.84 (1.93)
Hours Volunteering (per month)	10.50 (18.15)	9.70 (18.11)

Notes: Level of significance: $+\leq.10$; $*\leq.05$; $**\leq.01$; $***\leq.001$. Standard deviations in parentheses. Widows, N=51; wives, N=55.

hours of volunteering. More importantly, marriage increases group membership and reduces the hours of volunteering. Although these effects are in the predicted direction, neither of them is statistically significant.

Instead, what *does* appear to influence women's volunteerism are health, income, race, and hours helping friends. Older women who are in better health or in better financial shape belong to significantly more groups than do poorer or sicker women. Older women who are in better health and older women who are black also spend significantly more time volunteering than do their counterparts. Physical and material resources expand women's involvement in volunteer groups, while race and better health increase the intensity of their involvement in volunteer activities. More importantly, older women's resources are more important in shaping both the breadth and the depth of their volunteerism than is marriage.

Older women's friends also appear as an important motivation, increasing volunteerism. Hours spent helping friends have a strong positive effect on the number of groups to which women belong. Helping friends, of course, may be both a cause and a consequence of greater group membership. As we saw in Chapter 6, friends sometimes draw women into joining similar groups. Participating in volunteer activities also provides women opportunities to help their friends. In contrast, hours helping friends have no effect on the amount of time older women spend volunteering. Thus, while helping friends may increase

Table 9.2
OLS Regression of Number of Groups and Hours of Volunteering on Marital Status, Age, Health, Income, Employment, History of Help, and Race

Respondent Characteristics	Number of Groups	Hours of Volunteering[a]
Marriage[b]	-.19 (.44)	1.39 (4.24)
Age	.03 (.03)	-.10 (.25)
Health	-.35 (.20)+	-3.98 (1.94)*
Income[c]	.32 (1.50)*	5.73 (14.50)
History of Help	.05 (.07)	.81 (.69)
Race	-.42 (.49)	-10.58 (4.74)*
Employment[d]	.46 (.53)	-2.77 (5.07)
Care to Family[e]	-.20 (.34)	-4.04 (3.27)
Care to Friends[e]	4.08 (1.24) ***	-3.38 (1.19)
Constant	-.68 (1.99)	28.84 (19.20)
R^2	.26 (1.85)***	.11 (17.85)

Notes: Unstandardized beta coefficients (ß). Significance levels: $+\leq.10$; $*\leq.05$; $**\leq.01$; $***\leq.001$. Standard errors in parentheses. N=106.
[a] Hours volunteering per month. [b] Widowed=1; married=0.
[c] Family income in dollars, x 10,000. [d] Employed: yes=1; no=0.
[e] Hours per month helping family and friends x 100.

group membership, it does not increase the amount of time women spend volunteering.

Most importantly, although marriage may expand women's help to kin, this does not serve to integrate women into the larger community. The amount of time older women spend helping kin does not significantly affect either the number of groups joined or the number of hours spent volunteering. For these measures of participation, widows and wives are very much alike.

Marriage and Volunteering: Women's Words.   What the quantitative analysis somewhat obscures are the complex and contradictory effects of marriage on women's volunteerism. In fact, while *none* of these women talked about income as a reason for not volunteering, they *did* talk about the ways in which marriage both encouraged and discouraged their participation in volunteer associations.

A few husbands encouraged their wives' participation by volunteering themselves. Some husbands and wives were members of the same associations or belonged to the men's and women's branches of a larger organization. One woman who, like her husband, was active in several volunteer groups, wandered in toward the end of his interview and together they elaborated on their volunteering:

> *Mr. P.*: I've belonged to the Masons for years. My wife is also very active in the Eastern Star. The Masons is strictly a men's group, but their wives belong to the Eastern Star. It's not just an auxiliary, but the wives, daughters and mothers of the Masons. They have to have a Mason at each official meeting.
> *Mrs. P.*: I like it. So many young women are working and have no time to come. It takes many years to go through the different offices.
> *Mr. P.*: We get into something, and before you know it, we're officers.
> *Mrs. P.*:   We   used   to   teach   square   dancing.
> *Mr. P.*:   I used to call for four different clubs and they loved it. I'd do great calling jobs.
> *Mrs. P.*: All the groups we get in, we're active. We're doing a dog show up at the hospital this weekend.

This couple were obviously joiners, but more importantly, their comments illustrate how marriage draws women (and men) into volunteer activities in which they may become quite active. For this group, in particular, not only were wives dependent on husbands for membership, but women's meetings required at least one man to be in attendance. These couples (and these types of groups) were relatively rare, however, and most men and women who belong had been highly involved for many years. More frequently, husbands encouraged their wives' participation in other types of groups, perhaps to legitimize their own investment in the groups to which they belonged.

Women also related how husbands discourage their volunteering by preventing them from joining or by directly or indirectly influencing them to drop outside activities at a later date. Women who were responsible for the care of both husband and home often cut back on volunteering. One 79 year-old widow explained the history of her volunteerism this way: "Before my husband died, the only volunteer work I did was for church and my club. I'd do baking if they asked, but I didn't have time to do more." Similar stories were told by married women caring for husbands in poor health. "I don't do any volunteer work. I had to drop out when my husband got sick 2 years ago. With him and the house and doctor's appointments and trips to the drug store. You just don't know what's involved."

For some, this withdrawal was final—they no longer intend to volunteer. For others, withdrawal from volunteer activities was temporary. After a husband's death, some widows express renewed interest and involvement in volunteering: "I haven't belonged to any groups for two years. This year I haven't had the desire or ambition. This fall I'm going to do volunteer work. Not that I begrudge the care I gave John, but I'm not going to stay in the house. I was here enough. I feel now that I have the time to do more, that I should." By increasing the amount of routine housework and by requiring intensive care, ill husbands monopolize much of their wives' energy and indirectly discourage them from volunteering.

But husbands also have a more direct influence in limiting wives' volunteerism. Some think wives do too much outside the home and actively encourage them to do less.[2] In other cases, when husbands retire, wives reduce the amount of time they devote to volunteer work:

> I don't do a lot since my husband retired. I used to go to this nursing
> home and have a service there. I did it more before my husband was
> retired. I still visit shut-ins. It's not as scheduled as doing the service
> and I can do it whenever. I know people on the block who volunteer
> at the hospital, and I'd probably do that if I were alone, but I want to
> spend time with my husband.

Women's explanations for why they do, and do not, volunteer reveal some of the contradictory effects marriage has on volunteering—effects not seen in the quantitative analysis. Both directly and indirectly, husbands often limit wives' participation in volunteer activities. Some husbands, however, also promote wives' volunteerism either by encouraging them to join associations to which they themselves belong or by supporting their belonging to different volunteer groups. In these ways, marriage both pulls women into volunteering and pushes them out of it. More importantly, by doing both, marriage equalizes the involvement of widows and wives—an effect we see further in the types of groups to which older women belong.

Recipients of Care: Types of Groups

In general, married women belong to slightly more welfare, youth, job, veterans, political, ethnic, religious, community, and arts groups than do widows;

widows belong to the same number of service groups, slightly more groups for the elderly, and more recreational groups than do their married counterparts. However, it is only for political groups (.16 versus .02, p≤.05) that these differences are statistically significant—suggesting that husbands encourage their wives to be politically active or draw them into political groups by being active themselves.

Marriage, however, drops out even as a predictor of membership in political groups, when regression analysis is used to control for the effects of other variables on group membership (Table 9.3). Somewhat surprisingly, neither employment nor health has any effect on membership in any particular type of group. Instead, group memberships are most consistently affected by family income, race, prior history of helping others, and current hours of help to friends. Greater family income is particularly important in predicting membership in several types of groups. Women with higher income belong to more welfare, youth and political groups than do those with lower family income. Participation in youth oriented groups is also significantly affected by race: black women belong to significantly more youth groups than women who are white. This is consistent with Leslie Morgan's (1983) finding, that being black is positively associated with volunteering, in spite of its negative correlation with income (-.18, p=.033, in this sample). Age is only slightly related to participation in more service groups and may reflect a cohort difference in which older women belong to fraternal and service groups such as the Elks or Eastern Star. In addition, women with a greater history of helping family and friends belong to more recreational and more community groups than do those with less history of helping others.

Current involvement in helping family and friends also affects the types of groups to which older widows and wives belong. Overall, helping family tends to decrease membership in most types of groups. However, it is only for political groups that this relationship is significant—and there the relationship is weak, but positive. Women who spend more hours caring for family belong to more political groups than do other women. In contrast, helping friends has a strong positive effect on membership in several types of groups. Older women who spend more hours helping friends and neighbors belong to significantly more welfare groups, more groups for the elderly, and more religious groups than do older women who spend less time helping friends. It appears, then, that helping friends and helping others through volunteer associations are linked. Older women who spend more time helping friends are drawn into participation in more volunteer groups; at the same time the groups themselves provide women with greater opportunity to help their friends.

When women's other characteristics are taken into consideration, it is not marriage but the greater material and social resources marriage provides that increase married women's participation in political volunteer groups. Thus, while marriage does not directly increase wives' participation in political

Table 9.3
OLS Regression of Types of Groups on Marriage, Age, Health, Income, History of Help, Employment, and Race

	Welfare	Youth	Job	Veterans	Elderly	Political
Marriage	-.02 (.14)	.04 (.06)	-.04 (.06)	-.05 (.08)	.12 (.12)	.02 (.10)
Age	.02 (.01)	-.00 (.00)	.00 (.00)	-.00 (.00)	.00 (.01)	.00 (.01)
Health	-.09 (.07)	-.01 (.03)	-.01 (.03)	-.01 (.04)	.03 (.08)	-.00 (.04)
Income	1.01 (.49)*	.57 (.19)**	.03 (.20)	.26 (.28)	.74 (.59)	1.04 (.32)**
History of Help	-.00 (.02)	.01 (.01)	.01 (.01)	.01 (.01)	.02 (.03)	.00 (.02)
Race	.06 (.16)	-.21 (.06)***	-.02 (.07)	.04 (.09)	.07 (.19)	.06 (.11)
Employment	.25 (.17)	-.04 (.07)	.01 (.07)	.13 (.10)	.03 (.21)	.06 (.11)
Controls: Care to Kin	-.05 (.11)	.02 (.04)	.04 (.05)	-.00 (.06)	-.13 (.13)	.12 (.07)+
Care to Friends	1.47 (.41)***	-.13 (.15)	-.12 (.02)	.28 (.23)	1.36 (.49)**	-.15 (.03)
Constant	.79 (.65)	.14 (.25)	-.04 (.26)	.27 (.37)	-.05 (.78)	-.33 (.43)
R^2	.27 (.61)***	.22 (.23)**	.03 (.24)	.06 (.35)	.15 (.73)+	.19 (.40)*

Notes: Unstandardized beta coefficients (β). Symbols indicate significance levels: +$\leq$.10; *$\leq$.05; **$\leq$.01; ***$\leq$.001. N=106. See Table 9.2 for a description of these variables.

Table 9.3
(Continued)

	Ethnic	Service	Religious	Recreation	Community	Art/Cultural
Marriage	-.06 (.05)	-.05 (.06)	-.27 (.21)	.10 (.09)	-.02 (.03)	.01 (.08)
Age	.00 (.00)	.01 (.00)+	.01 (.01)	-.00 (.01)	.00 (.00)	.00 (.01)
Health	.01 (.02)	-.02 (.02)	-.13 (.09)	-.07 (.04)	-.01 (.02)	-.05 (.03)
Income	-.00 (.16)	.00 (.19)	-.54 (.70)	-.11 (.31)	.15 (.11)	.40 (.25)
History of Help	.00 (.01)	.00 (.01)	-.05 (.03)	.05 (.02)**	.01 (.01)*	-.02 (.01)
Race	-.07 (.05)	-.02 (.06)	-.29 (.23)	.05 (.10)	-.05 (.04)	.02 (.08)
Employment	.03 (.06)	-.05 (.07)	.02 (.25)	-.03 (.11)	.01 (.04)	.06 (.09)
Controls:						
Care to Kin	-.04 (.04)	-.02 (.04)	.13 (.16)	-.09 (.07)	-.03 (.02)	-.06 (.05)
Care to Friends	-.08 (.01)	.20 (.02)	1.30 (5.80)*	.01 (.26)	-.09 (.09)	.05 (.21)
Constant	-.04 (.21)	-.33 (.25)	.47 (.93)	.29 (.41)	.01 (.14)	-.14 (.34)
R²	.07 (.19)	.19 (.23)	.11 (.87)	.17 (.38)*	.12 (.13)	.11 (.31)

Notes: Unstandardized beta coefficients (β). Symbols indicate significance levels: $+ \leq .10$; $* \leq .05$; $** \leq .01$; $*** \leq .001$. N=106. See Table 9.2 for a description of these variables.

organizations, it may indirectly have the same effect by increasing family income and expanding networks of kin to whom wives give help—through whom they may be drawn into political volunteer activities. In most cases, however, marriage makes little difference in the types of groups to which older women belong.[3]

Employment, Child Rearing and Volunteerism: Women's Words. Athough the quantitative analysis suggests marriage itself has very little effect on volunteer group membership, the women in this study often spoke at length about the history of their volunteerism and clearly linked participation in different types of groups to their position in the life course. Although some characterized themselves as never having been "joiners," most had been involved in a number of groups in the past and had dropped some or exchanged them for others over time. These were mostly age specific groups—groups women linked to particular periods in their life histories. Groups such as the Scouts, PTA, Little League, and many religious organizations are associated with a time when these women were married and heavily involved in child rearing. Membership in these groups is no longer relevant.

Others related how volunteering and employment were part of a sequential pattern in much the same way that child rearing and employment are sequential activities among younger women: "A group of us were involved and did all types of projects. I was a member until we all got full time jobs 6 years ago. Then we were employed; there just wasn't enough time because I was exhausted. Then, after retiring, we got back together." The general outline that emerges from these discussions is that volunteering and child rearing went hand-in-hand for many of these women. In some cases employment replaced both—as women with grown children took jobs. In these cases, children, like friends, integrate women into volunteer groups in a way that marriage does not.

Charity Work

Not all volunteer groups or time spent volunteering helps the needy. Within groups that do help the needy, are married women more likely to be involved than widows? Or do widowed women, women whose energies are less absorbed by caring for a husband and a home, assume a greater burden of caring for those in need outside the home—the needy who are neither family nor friends?

Table 9.4 compares the percentage of widows and wives who help four types of needy people—the poor, sick, elderly, or other needy groups.[4] In general, married women are slightly more likely to participate in groups that help those in need than are widows. The percentage of married women who participate in groups that help the needy ranges from 55 to 60 percent, while the percentage of widows who help the needy ranges from 39 to 55 percent. These

Table 9.4
Charity Work by Widows and Wives
(t-Tests)

I. % Who Help	Married Women	Widowed Women
The Poor	.58 (1.30)	.43 (.88)
The Sick	.55 (1.27)	.43 (.76)
The Elderly	.58 (1.26)	.55 (.97)
Other Needy	.60 (1.33)	.39 (.92)
TOTAL: The Poor, Sick, Elderly or Other Needy People[a]	1.01 (1.58)	.75 (1.21)
II. Hours Helping (mean)		
The Poor	54.2 (147.39)	40.4 (118.49)
The Sick	46.2 (127.94)	55.3 (136.06)
The Elderly	47.2 (128.84)	68.9 (153.67)
Other Needy	53.3 (145.11)	63.8 (182.25)
TOTAL: The Poor, Sick, Elderly, or Other Needy People[b]	86.0 (189.50)	97.2 (215.19)

Notes: Level of significance: $+\leq.10$; $*\leq.05$; $**\leq.01$; $***\leq.001$. Standard deviations in parentheses. Widows, N=51; Wives, N=55. [a] Since each group may help more than one type of needy persons, mean scores may be greater than 1. [b] Hours spent last year helping each group of needy persons may overlap (e.g., hours to poor, may also have been hours to the sick).

differences, however, are not statistically significant.

Table 9.4 also compares the hours widows and wives spend helping different types of needy people. While married women spend more hours working with volunteer groups that help the poor, widows spend more hours working with volunteer groups that help the sick, elderly or other needy—as well as more hours helping the needy overall. Again, however, these differences are not statistically significant. Both widowed and married women spend 4 to 5 hours a month volunteering to help the needy. Widows spend essentially no more time helping the needy than do wives. In fact, even when factors shown to affect more general participation in volunteer groups are controlled for, neither marriage nor any of these other variables has a significant effect on the amount of time older women spend doing traditional charity work.[5]

Overall, these findings suggest marriage does not significantly affect older women's involvement in traditional charity work. The shrinking family responsibilities that accompany widowhood do not necessarily result in greater help to strangers in need—a disappointment for those promoting greater volunteerism among the elderly as a means of supplementing programs of public welfare.[6]

Widows and Wives as Volunteers

What about the women who *do* volunteer? What is the work of volunteering that older women perform? And how is that labor affected by marriage?

Table 9.5 compares the tasks performed by married and widowed women as volunteers who spend 50 or more hours a year working with a particular association. The majority of highly involved volunteers concentrate their efforts in providing direct care to those in need, supervising other volunteers, fund-raising, acting as speaker for the group, and telephoning. Fifty-seven percent of highly involved widows and 39 percent of the wives give direct care to those in need. Second only to direct care is telephoning (50 percent of the wives, and 36 percent of the widows), followed by fund- raising (17 percent for wives and 29 percent for widows), speaking for the group (33 percent for wives and 21 percent for widows), and recruiting new members (33 percent among wives, compared with only 7 percent among widows). Both providing care to those in need and maintaining and coordinating their fellow volunteers are central to older women's work as volunteers.

Whether, and in what ways, widows and wives differ in this work is also seen in Table 9.5. Married women are slightly more likely to supervise other volunteers, organize meetings, act as speaker, recruit new members, and do telephoning than are widows. In contrast, widowed women are slightly more likely to act as treasurers and secretaries, do fund-raising, preside over meetings, and write letters for the groups in which they are highly involved. It is only in recruiting new members, however, that these differences reach statistical significance. On almost every task, widows and wives are very much alike.[7]

Table 9.5
Tasks Married Women and Widows Perform for High-Involvement Groups
(Chi-Square)

	Percent Doing Each Task	
Type of volunteer help	Married	Widowed
Direct Care	.39 (.50)	.57 (.51)
Treasurer	.06 (.24)	.14 (.36)
Supervise Volunteers	.28 (.46)	.21 (.43)
Fund Raising	.17 (.38)	.29 (47)
Organize Meetings	.22 (.43)	.07 (.27)
Speaker	.33 (.49)	.21 (.43)
Presider	.17 (.38)	.29 (.47)
Write Letters	.06 (.24)	.07 (.27)
Recruit Members	.33 (.49)	.07 (.27)*
Secretary	.17 (.38)	.21 (.43)
Telephone	.50 (.51)	.36 (.50)
Other	.06 (.24)	.07 (.27)

Notes: Level of significance: $+ \leq .10$; $* \leq .05$; $** \leq .01$; $*** \leq .001$. Widows, N=14; wives, N=18. Standard deviations in parentheses. All figures are per month, for highly involved women (50+hours of volunteering per month).

When other key characteristics are controlled for, marriage only significantly affects women's acting as presider over group meetings. Widows are slightly more likely to preside over the meetings of groups with which they are highly involved than are their married counterparts. Along with age and less history of help, marriage tends to inhibit older women from assuming what is often a more time consuming responsibility within volunteer organizations.[8]

SUMMARY AND DISCUSSION

In general, marriage has very limited effects on older women's volunteering. Both the breadth of women's volunteerism, in terms of number of groups, and the depth of their involvement—whether hours of participation or the types of work they do as volunteers—are largely unaffected by whether or not they are married. Both widows and wives belong to similar numbers of groups and spend similar amounts of time volunteering.

Other than increasing wives' participation in political groups—a reflection, perhaps, of their husbands' own involvement, but also of their income—marriage has no effect on the types of groups to which women belong. Instead, position in the life course (in terms of completed child rearing and employment), as well as current financial and physical resources, affect older women's volunteerism—whether type or number of groups, or hours of volunteering—more than marriage itself.

Widowhood clearly reintegrates women into networks of friends to whom they give care (Chapter 7). Yet, widowhood does not translate into greater help to others through volunteer efforts. Rather, older women's volunteerism is a more complicated matter. It is shaped by women's history of involvement in helping others, attitudes toward work, and health, as well as husband's (or late husband's) attitudes toward their volunteering. Women who are volunteers—who have a long history of volunteering at each stage of their lives—are women who continue to look for ways to volunteer in spite of declining health and abilities. Other women, some of whom were also volunteers, argue that they've done their share; they are no longer interested in volunteering, and resist being made to feel they ought to do more. In these ways, both disengagement and continuity characterize older widows' and wives' formal help to others.

Nevertheless, this analysis provides some evidence that marriage both encourages and restricts older women's volunteerism. Some of this is in the form of women's discussions of the history of their volunteerism—how they participated over the years with husbands in joint volunteer activities, or how a husband's illness absorbed much of the energy or time that was once spent caring for others, or how a husband's retirement meant more time at home and less ability to commit themselves to scheduled or structured volunteering.

While the quantitative analysis may obscure the direct "push-pull" of marriage on older women's volunteerism, what the quantitative analysis *does* show are the indirect effects marriage has on the types of groups to which older women belong. Marriage indirectly increases participation in some groups while decreasing participation in others. So, too, it both expands and restricts older women's help to family and friends—those through whom they may be drawn into a range of volunteer activities.

NOTES

1. Although the correlation between age and employment is significant (p=.001), multicollinearity is not likely to be a problem because the correlation is not high (-.38). No substantial differences appear in the regression analysis when age and employment are alternately omitted from or added to the equations.

2. Only 4.2 percent of the married women thought that they did too much volunteer work, while 19 percent reported that their husbands thought they did too much. Contrasting this with husbands' attitudes toward the help their wives give relatives; 7 percent of the women reported their husband thought they did too much for their adult children and 5.6 percent reported that their husband thought they did too much for other relatives. In general, then, husbands appear to be more disapproving of wives' helping nonkin than they are of their wives' helping kin.

3. While marriage may indirectly increase older women's membership in political groups through extending women's help to kin, it may indirectly decrease participation in other types of groups by limiting networks of friends.

4. Compared with women under the age of 60, these older women are similarly involved in groups that help the needy (40.6 percent for the older sample, 42.7 percent for the younger sample). Although these data are not longitudinal, they do suggest a strong continuity in women's charity work into old age.

5. Only race significantly affects the hours older women devote to helping those in need who are neither family nor friends. Black women spend more time helping other types of needy people than do women who are white. Since young people were not specified as a group of needy, black women's greater hours of help to "other" needy (not the poor, sick or elderly) may reflect high participation in youth oriented groups (see Table 9.4). When hours of help to all types of needy are combined, women who are black, as well as women who are in better health spend more hours helping the needy overall than do their counterparts (data not shown).

6. In fact, among some women there is explicit resistance to the notion that they form a pool of potential volunteers. One retired woman spoke at length about her resistance to being recruited as a volunteer:

> After I retired, people said, "Don't you want to do this?" and I said, no. And they said, "Don't you want to do this?" and I said, no. Agencies just felt that I really wasn't doing anything but sitting around eating bon-bons, and therefore was an untapped source of manpower. And I feel I've done my share. [Interviewer, "What kinds of groups called you?"] Any kind, Red Cross, you name it. I think they probably called everybody on the street. I think they had my name from this source or

that source, or whatever, and just felt that I'm free, I'm at their disposal. And I still, I go back to the fact that I've done my share. I enjoyed it while I was doing it, but I don't want to do it now. I'm not doing it because I don't want to. I've worked very hard, not always for pay. This is the time in life where I'll do what I please, and I'll do as much or as little of it as I please. And as far as looking at the retired, the community, as an untapped source of manpower, they're wrong. We're not going to do it. And we're not going to do it because we don't want to.

Some women, then, expressly linked being recruited as a volunteer to public policy. Even among those who did not, however, a recurring theme as women discussed their volunteerism was "I've done my share." Although some women anticipated "getting back into volunteer work" after retiring, the majority resisted being made to feel obligated to volunteer. In these ways, those most able in terms of available time, if not always physical or material resources, may not be among those most responsive to programs recruiting "new" old volunteers.

7. The numbers of groups for which widows and wives perform these tasks are only slightly different. Married women do recruiting and more telephoning for significantly more groups than do widows.

8. Apart from presiding over group meetings, neither together nor individually is marriage or women's other characteristics particularly useful in predicting the tasks older widows and wives do as volunteers. There are only three exceptions. Women who are in better health act as secretaries and do other group tasks (not specified during the interviews), while employed women write letters, and women who are younger act as group speakers more than their older, nonemployed or less healthy counterparts (data not shown).

Part IV

Conclusions

10

The Implications of Giving Care: Labors of Love and Responsibility

INTRODUCTION

Caring and giving care are inextricably entwined, as the work involved in helping others and feelings of affection for those one helps often (but not always) go hand-in-hand. Yet, the men and women interviewed for this study both recognized and articulated this distinction between labor and love, caring and giving care. In most cases, older men's and women's reasons for helping others were easily and readily explained in terms of love and the responsibility that love entailed. The actual labor involved, on the other hand, was often more of a labor to recall. Once articulated, however, the time and tasks that go into helping others were clearly distinguished from the emotions that accompanied them. Caring for others is labor—albeit, labors of love.

Perhaps one of the reasons this labor goes unnoticed (until a sociologist prompts you to remember) is because its invisibility helps to maintain, and is maintained by, the ideological distinction between labor and love. Because this is a culture in which work and family, labor and emotion are separated, detailing the time and tasks that go into helping others underscores this otherwise muted distinction. It goes against the grain of understanding caring as being based on love and affection, rather than action. Moreover, labors of love "belong" to actors in a way that much other labor does not, since feelings, whether of love or responsibility, remain largely outside the cash economy.[1] We may readily sell our time or our labor, but not our feelings. The little things done for others may be valuable, then, not because they have great cash value, but precisely because they do not. To recognize the time and tasks involved in giving care, to articulate the work involved in helping others, begins to put too much of an economic face on this labor and runs the risk of robbing it of some of its worth.

The work involved in giving care also is unnoticed because it is so much a part of the ebb and flow of daily life. Yet, unnoticed is not the same as unimportant. It is the "nothings" that make up a large part of the help men and women give others from which community arises and through which it is maintained. Sociological analyses of interaction and those that focus primarily on care received tend to miss this point. By concentrating on contact or on how the needs of particularly dependent others are met, these studies neglect the ways in which exchanges of everyday help and support build and maintain community—whether among families, friends, or others. Yet this labor is fundamental, even essential, to social life.

What is the work of caring, then, that older men and women, widows and wives, do? And what does this labor tell us about how social life is organized around the twin constructs of gender and marriage?

GENDER AND GIVING CARE

This analysis helps to specify the ways in which gender shapes community and social integration. Older women are clearly more embedded in caring relations than are older men. They spend more time and provide more types of help to a larger number of kin and a larger number of people overall than do older men. This embeddedness in caring is especially seen in the amount of time older women spend helping others. Married women over 60 spend more than 50 hours a month helping kin, almost 7 hours a month helping friends and neighbors, and more than 10 hours a month volunteering (most of which is spent in activities that help those in need). The number of hours older women spend helping others clearly reveals something of their commitment to their roles as kinkeepers, friend keepers, and volunteers. Making this invisible labor visible also demonstrates the centrality of women to the maintenance of both families and communities.

Older women are not only more embedded than older men in caring relations, they also help more extended networks of people than do older men. In particular, older women help more people overall, as well as more kin, than older men. Older women's helping networks are thus more expansive than older men's—with two important exceptions. Older women do not help a larger number of their own kin, nor do they help a larger number of friends than do older men.

These exceptions help to specify the meaning of women's embeddedness. While some theorists argue women's giving care reflects "essential" differences between women and men, differences rooted in psychosocial development and a uniquely female morality, this analysis shows that older women are not more connected than men in some general, overarching way. Rather, opportunities and resources, as well as personal predispositions for giving care, help to shape what and to whom older men and women give care. Marriage, in particular, creates opportunities for greater help to kin for both older women and men. Yet, these opportunities translate into greater caring for older women more than for older men.

In addition, although current employment does not significantly affect the size of the networks of friends and neighbors older men and women help, differences in employment history may mean older men have had greater opportunity to establish relations with nonkin, relations through which helping friends may persist beyond retirement into old age. While the qualitative analysis presented here hints at the importance of work history in shaping help given to nonkin, this question would be better addressed through an analysis of longitudinal, rather than cross-sectional data.

Perhaps more importantly, this analysis specifies the ways in which older men's and women's personal resources affect what and to whom they give help. Not surprisingly, income is a particularly salient variable affecting the number and types of tasks older men and women do for people they know. When income is not controlled for, older women do more practical and personal tasks for family and friends than do older men. When family income is taken into account, however, we find older women do more material tasks than men as well. The effects of income suggest women's caring is not merely a reflection of essential gender differences that make them more responsive, more connected to the needs of others. Rather, patterns of care also reflect larger social-structural factors that affect older men's and women's ability to help others.

At best, this analysis provides only minimal support for those theories that argue for a uniquely female ethic of care. Instead, this analysis shows that both older men and older women help others in need. Whether to kin in general, adult children, or friends and neighbors, older women's caring is essentially no more linked to the needs of those they help than is older men's. Nor are there significant gender differences in helping other groups of needy who are neither family nor friends. In fact, the only instances where the help older women give is more closely linked to the needs of the recipients are giving more personal help to kin overall and helping adult daughters who may be in greater financial need.

Older women, then, are not simply more connected or responsive to others in a way that older men are not, but are rational actors whose giving care is shaped by their ability to provide care, as well as the needs of those they help.

Finally, regarding gender, this study reveals something of the nature of the help older men and women give. Two findings are particularly important in this regard. First, older women spend more time and perform a greater number of tasks than older men. Second, older women's help is no more linked to the needs of those they help than is older men's. In fact, for helping kin in general and for helping friends, older *men's* help is more linked to the needs of the recipients than is older women's. Together, these findings suggest that the help older women give family and friends consists more of everyday expressions of help and support, while the help older men give family and friends consists more of actions or gifts intended to meet specific, perhaps acute needs. Moreover, these findings show that part of what may be initially taken for gender differences is in fact differences in access and control over the resources which make caring possible. This idea is further supported in the findings on patterns of help given by older widows and wives.

MARRIAGE AND GIVING CARE

Along with gender, this study helps to specify the ways in which marriage shapes the help older women give others. On the one hand, marriage clearly integrates older women into relations of helping kin that are remarkably unaffected by loss of spouse. While married women help more kin, whether related by blood or by marriage, than do widows, this difference can be explained in terms of differences in family income, age, and employment, rather than marriage itself. When these other social-structural factors are controlled for, married and widowed women do not differ in the number of kin helped. Marriage, then, expands the number of kin to whom older women provide care, regardless of whether the caregiver is currently married or widowed. Although these data are not longitudinal, these findings do suggest that the power of marriage to expand women's kinkeeping continues even after the loss of a husband.

In contrast, marriage increases the intensity of older women's helping relations with kin. Even when other social-structural factors are introduced, wives spend more than 24 hours more a month helping kin than do widows. Perhaps older women's commitment to helping kin declines after widowhood. At the very least, while married and widowed women help similarly extended networks of kin, widows are less embedded in intensive caring relations with kin than are wives.

Helping friends and neighbors is a different story. In direct contrast to the effects of marriage on older women's helping kin, marriage clearly restricts older women's help to friends and neighbors. Whether in terms of hours of care or numbers helped, widows are more involved in helping friends than are wives. In spite of the fact that widows tend to be older, to have poorer health, and to have significantly lower family income, widows spend more time helping more friends than women who are married. At a stage, then, when older women seem to disengage from their commitment to helping kin, widowed women reengage in helping friends and neighbors.

Studies which argue that marriage is a greedy institution and those which argue that it is a powerful integrating institution are both partially correct. Marriage clearly integrates women into expanded networks of kin to whom they provide care—relations that seem to persist, to some extent, after the loss of a husband. However, marriage is also greedy and restricts both the breadth and depth of help older women give friends and neighbors.

Marriage is greedy not only as an institution, however. The findings presented here also suggest that husbands themselves limit the types of help and support older women give others—whether kin or nonkin. This is most clearly seen in the types of help widows and wives give in response to the material needs of others, and in the help widows give unmarried sons. Widowed women give more material help—whether gifts, goods, or money—to poorer kin and friends than to their wealthier counterparts; wives give not more money, but more comfort and advice. In addition, widowed women give more of each type of help and support to unmarried sons than to their married counterparts, while a son's marriage has no effect on the help older still married mothers provide. It appears, then, that widowed women transfer some of the help given to husbands to sons without wives.

In these ways, husbands themselves—as well as marriage as an institution—shape older women's informal help to family and friends. While widows may have fewer resources on which to draw in helping others, they seem to have more say about how those resources are used in meeting others' needs.

Finally, this analysis helps to specify the ways in which marriage both encourages and discourages older women's volunteerism. It directly encourages volunteerism through increasing participation in couples oriented groups. Marriage also indirectly increases older women's volunteerism by expanding help to kin, who, in turn, draw women into particular types of volunteer groups. At the same time, marriage directly and indirectly restricts older women's volunteerism. It absorbs their energies and time through focusing their caring on retired or sick husbands. It also restricts older women's involvement in helping friends—friends who, in turn, might draw them into greater participation in volunteer activities.

THE NEW VOLUNTEERS?

Along with the implications of these findings for theories of gender and marriage, this study has practical implications. In an effort to further privatize both family and community care, over the past decade the state has revitalized its interest in promoting volunteerism, particularly among older, retired Americans. This is, in effect, asking women, once again, to do the work of providing care. The women in this study have done this all their lives—and most of them resist the suggestion that they should pick up where the state has left off caring for those in need. They resist, both implicitly in describing how they've "learned to say no", and explicitly in rejecting the notion that they are a source of free help and support within the community. As a result, there may be little response to calls for renewed volunteerism among the elderly.

For some women, volunteering is a way to stay involved—both after retirement, and, for widows, after the death of a spouse. Most, however, felt they had done their share of formal volunteer work, and some resented being treated as a source of free labor.

SUGGESTIONS FOR FUTURE RESEARCH

Because this analysis is based on a relatively small sample of respondents, interviewed at one point in time, there are clear limits to how it can be used in analyzing the effects of age, widowhood, and retirement on older men's and women's giving care. As suggested at several points, some of these questions would be better answered by using longitudinal, rather than cross-sectional, data. Moreover, because of the relatively small sample, comparable analyses of a larger sample of respondents might reveal greater differences by gender or marriage than were found here. Although the time and cost involved in following a cohort of men and women through adulthood into old age may be prohibitive, a longitudinal analysis following a larger cohort of respondents (including widowers) would allow a more detailed examination of the relationships among widowhood, retirement and giving care.

In spite of the constraints associated with cross-sectional research, this study provides some indication of the importance of other social-structural factors that, along with gender, help to shape what and to whom older men and women, widows and wives give care. Furthermore, it demonstrates the centrality of older women's caring to the maintenance and well-being of both families and communities. But this labor has implications for the well-being of caregivers as well. Although the greater burden of care falls on women than on men, women's embeddedness in giving care may result in greater benefit to them, as adult children "pay back" help received over the years. This idea finds support in recent work on parent-child relations, which finds that older women benefit more than older men from their investment in caring for children (Spitze and Logan, 1989). This trend may extend to older women's helping others as well, as both family and friends reciprocate the help and support they have received.

Older women's commitment to helping others may also result in greater psychological or physiological distress among older women than among older men. While this analysis has not dealt with the mental health or physiological outcomes of older men's and women's giving care, these are issues that should be, and are being, addressed elsewhere.[2]

There are, not surprisingly, a number of additional questions this study raises but does not pursue. In particular, examining patterns of help by race, as well as gender, may provide additional support for the role of structural resources in affecting what and to whom care is given. In addition, this analysis contains hints of gender differences in motivations for helping family and friends (as well as differences in motivations for helping different types of recipients). Yet, these, too, may be related to other social-structural forces such as class or income, rather than gender itself. Finally, this study points to the importance of linking informal help to family and friends with help given others through formal volunteer efforts. These connections have important implications not only for public policy intended to increase volunteerism among the elderly but for theories of gender, marriage, and aging as well.

NOTES

1. Feelings are one of the few aspects of life that have not been absorbed by Braverman's "universal market" (1974), yet as Hochschild points out (1983), some occupations require emotional labor, as well as physical or intellectual labor.

2. Some of this work is being done. A recent study by Pillemer and Suitor (1991) finds little gender difference in parental distress associated with caring for adult children. Other work on younger and middle aged adults finds non-normative care increases distress among women, while most types of caring increase distress among men (Gerstel and Gallagher, 1990b).

Appendix: Letters to Respondents

Dear Mrs. Jones,

Thank you for speaking with us concerning the study I am doing of family and community life in Springfield. I would very much like to talk to you and appreciate your willingness to consider participation in this study. Let me anticipate a few questions you might have.

I am interested in how people's relationships with family, friends and neighbors change as people get older. I'm sure that you have experienced some of these changes yourself, and I would love to talk with you about your own experiences with neighbors, friends, relatives and community organizations. Since each person's experience is unique, it's important that I talk with a wide variety of people, including yourself. Each interview is completely confidential.

This study is being conducted under the auspices of the Department of Sociology at the University of Massachusetts at Amherst. We are *not* a marketing research firm, nor are we involved with trying to market any product.

I am conducting all of these interviews myself, and can come to Springfield at any time that is convenient for you—days, evenings, or weekends. Or, if you prefer, you may come to my office here in Amherst.

Thank you for your consideration. I appreciate your willingness to allow me to write to you personally, and look forward to speaking with you soon.

Sincerely,

Sally Gallagher

P.S. Either I or a member of our staff will call again next week to see if we can arrange a convenient time to meet with you. If you prefer, you may call me collect at the above number to set up a time for an interview.

Dear Mrs. Jones,

Thank you for agreeing to participate in the study of family and community life I am conducting in Springfield. As we agreed when we spoke on the phone yesterday, I will be coming down to Springfield to talk with you on Thursday, June 30, at 1:30.

I look forward to meeting you then.

Sincerely,

Sally Gallagher

Bibliography

Abel, E. 1990. *Who cares for the elderly? Public policy and the experience of adult daughters*. Philadelphia: Temple University Press.

Abel, E. 1986. Adult daughters and care for the elderly. *Feminist Studies*. 12: 479-497.

ACTION. 1975. *Americans volunteer — 1974: A statistical study of volunteers in the United States*. Washington, DC: ACTION.

Adams, B. 1970. Isolation, function, and beyond: American kinship in the 1960's. *Journal of Marriage and the Family*. 32: 575-597.

Adams, B. 1968. *Kinship in an Urban Setting*. Chicago: Markham.

Adams, R. G. 1987. Patterns of network change: A longitudinal study of friendships of elderly women. *The Gerontologist*. 27: 222-227.

Adams, R. G. & Blieszner, R. 1989. *Older adult friendship*. Newbury Park, CA: Sage.

Ahrons, C.R. & Bowman, M.E. 1982. Changes in family relationships following the divorce of a adult child: Grandmothers perceptions. *Journal of Divorce*. 5: 49-68.

Aldous, J. 1987. New views on the family life of the elderly and the near-elderly. *Journal of Marriage and the Family*. 49: 227-234.

Aldous, J. 1985. Parent-adult child relations as affected by grandparent status. In V. Bengtson & J. Robertson (Eds.), *Grandparenthood*. Beverly Hills, CA: Sage.

Aldous, J. & Hulsman, J. 1986. Relationships between parents and their adult children: Does retirement make a difference? Paper presented at the Annual Meeting of the National Council on Family Relations, November.

Aldous, J. & Straus, M. A. 1966. Social networks and conjugal roles: A test of Botts hypothesis. *Social Forces*. 44: 576-580.

Altergott, K. 1985. Marriage, gender, and social relations in late life. In W. Peterson & J. Quadangno (Eds.), *Social bonds in later life: Aging and interdependence.* Beverly Hills, CA: Sage.

Altergott, K. & Duncan, S. 1987. Age, gender and activities of daily life. Paper presented at the Annual Meeting of the Gerontological Society, Washington, DC.

Antonucci, T, & Akiyama, H. 1987. Social networks in adult life and a preliminary examination of the convoy model. *Journal of Gerontology, 42,* 519-27.

Anderson, T. 1984. Widowhood as a life transition: Its impact on kinship ties. *Journal of Marriage and the Family, 46,* 105-114.

Arling, G. 1976. The elderly widow and her family, neighbors and friends. *Journal of Marriage and the Family, 38,* 757-768.

Atchley, R. C. 1989. A continuity theory of normal aging. *The Gerontologist, 29,* 183-190.

Atchley, R. C. 1985. *Social forces and aging: An introduction to social gerontology.* Belmont, California: Wadsworth.

Atchley, R. C. 1975. Dimensions of widowhood in later life. *The Gerontologist, 15,* 76-177.

Atchley, R. C. 1975. *The effect of marital status on social interaction patterns of older women.* Oxford, Ohio: Scripps Foundation.

Atchley, R. C. & Miller, J. S. 1980. Older people and their families. In C. Eisdorfer (Ed.), *American review of gerontology and geriatrics.* New York: Springer Publishing.

Atchley, R. C., Pignatello, L. & Shaw, E. 1979. Interactions with family and friends: Marital status and occupations differences among older women. *Research on Aging, 1,* 83-95.

Babchuk, N. 1979. Primary ties of aged men. Paper presented at the Thirty-Second Meeting of the Gerontological Society, Washington, DC, November.

Babchuk, N. 1978. Aging and primary relations. *International Journal of Aging and Human Development, 9,* 137-151.

Babchuck, N. & Anderson, T. B. 1989. Older widows and married women: Their intimates and confidants. *International Journal of Aging and Human Development, 28,* 21-35.

Babchuk, N. & Booth, A. 1969. Voluntary association membership: A longitudinal analysis. *American Sociological Review, 34,* 31-45.

Babchuk, N., Peters, G. R., Hoyt, D. R. & Kaiser, M. A. 1979. The voluntary associations of the aged. *Journal of Gerontology, 34,* 579-587.

Bacharack, C. A. 1980. Childlessness and social isolation among the elderly. *Journal of Marriage and the Family, 42,* 627-637.

Bahr, H. 1976. The kinship role. In F. I. Nye (Ed.), *Role structure and analysis of the family*. Beverly Hills, California: Sage.

Baire, A. 1985. What do women want in a moral theory? *Nous, 19*, 53-64.

Bankoff, E. A. 1983. Social support and adaptation to widowhood. *Journal of Marriage and the Family, 45*, 226-230.

Bankoff, E. A. 1984. Aged parents and their widowed daughters: A support relationship. *Journal of Gerontology, 39*, 230-239.

Barusch, A. S. & Spain, W. 1989. Gender differences in caregiving: Why do wives report greater burden? *The Gerontologist, 29*, 667-676.

Beck, S. & Beck, R. 1984. The formation of extended households during middle age. *Journal of Marriage and the Family, 46*, 277-287.

Beckman, L. J & Houser, B. B. 1982. The consequences of childlessness on the social and psychological well-being of older women. *Journal of Gerontology, 37*, 243-250.

Bell, W. & Force, M. T. 1956. Urban neighborhood types and participation in formal associations. *American Sociological Review, 21*, 25-34.

Bengtson, V. L. 1985. Diversity and symbolism and grandparental roles. In V. L. Bengtson & J. F. Robertson (Eds.), *Grandparenthood*. Beverly Hills, California: Sage.

Bengtson, V. L. & Robertson, J. F. 1985. *Grandparenthood*. Beverly Hills, California: Sage Publications.

Bengtson, V. L. & Schrader, S. J. 1982. Parent-child relations: The measurement of intergenerational interaction and affection in old age. In D. Mangen & W. Peterson (Eds.), *Handbook of Research Instruments in Social Gerontology, Volume One: Clinical and Social Psychology*. Minneapolis, Minnesota: University of Minnesota Press.

Berardo, E. 1970. Survivorship and social isolation: The case of the aged widower. *The Family Coordinator, 19*, 11-25.

Berardo, E. 1968. Widowhood status in the U.S.: Perspectives on a neglected aspect of the family life cycle. *The Family Coordinator, 17*, 191-203.

Berk, S. F. 1988. Women's unpaid labor: Home and community. In A. Stromberg & S. Harkess (Eds.). *Women working*. CA: Mayfield.

Bernard, J. 1976. *The future of motherhood*. New York: Penguin.

Bernard, J. 1973. *The future of marriage*. New York: Bantum.

Beyer, G. & Woods M. 1963. Living and activity patterns of the aged. Research Report No. 6, Ithaca, New York: Center for Housing and Environmental Studies, Cornell University. In M. Riley & A. Foner (Eds.), *Aging and Society*. New York: Russel Sage.

Birren, J. E. & Renner, V. J. 1977. Research on the psychology of aging and principles of experimentation. In J. E. Birren & K. W. Schaie (Eds.), *Handbook on the psychology of aging*. New York: Van Nostrand-Reinhold.

Birren, J. & Schaie, K. W. 1985. *Handbook of the psychology of aging*. New York: Van Nostrand-Reinhold.

Blau, Z. S. 1973. *Old age in changing society*. New York: New Viewpoints.

Blau, Z. S. 1961. Structural constraints on friendship in old age. *American Sociological Review, 26*, 429-439.

Booth, A. 1972. Sex and social participation. *American Sociological Review, 37*, 183-192.

Bott, E. 1955. Urban families: Conjugal roles and social networks. *Human Relations, 8*, 345-384.

Brabeck, M. M. 1989. *Who cares? Theory, research and educational implications of the ethic of care*. New York: Praeger.

Braverman, H. 1974. *Labor and monopoly capital: The degradation of work in the twentieth century*. New York: Monthly Review Press.

Brody, E. 1990. *Women in the middle: Their parent care years*. New York: Springer.

Brody, E. 1985. Parent care as normative family stress. *The Gerontologist, 25*, 19-29.

Brody, E. 1981. Women in the middle and family support to older people. *The Gerontologist, 21*, 471-480.

Brody, E. 1978. The aging of the family. *The Annals, 197*, 12-21.

Brody, E., Kleban, M., Johnsen, P., Hoffmen, C. & Schoonover, C. 1987. Work status and parent care: A comparison of four groups of women. *The Gerontologist, 27*, 201-208.

Brody, E. M. & Schoonover, C. B. 1986. Patterns of parent-care when adult daughters work and when they do not. *The Gerontologist, 26*, 372-381.

Brody, E., Johnsen, P. & Fulcomer, M. 1984. What should adult children do for elderly parents? Opinions and preferences of three generations of women. *Journal of Gerontology, 39*, 736-746.

Brody, E., Johnsen, P., Fulcomer, M. & Lang, A. 1983. Women's changing roles and help to elderly parents: Attitudes of three generations of women. *Journal of Gerontology, 38*, 596-607.

Brown, B. B. 1981. A life-span approach to friendship: Age-related dimensions on an ageless relationship. In H. Z. Lopata & D. Maines (Eds.), *Research in the interweave of social roles: Friendship* (Vol. 2). Greenwich, CT: JAI Press.

Brown, Richard D. 1973. The emergence of voluntary associations in massachusetts, 1760-1830. *Journal of Voluntary Action Research, 2*, 64-73.

Brubaker, T. 1989. Families in later life: A burgeoning research area. *Journal of Marriage and the Family, 52*, 959-981.

Brubaker, T. & Hennon, C. B. 1982. Responsibility for household tasks: Comparing dual earner and dual retired marriages. In M. Szinovacz (Ed.), *Women's retirement: Policy implications of recent research.* Beverly Hills, CA: Sage.

Brumberg, J. J. 1980. Benevolent beginnings: Volunteer traditions among American women, 1800-1860. In United Hospital Fund, *Women, volunteering, and health policy.* New York: United Hospital Fund of New York.

Bull, C. N. 1982. Voluntary associations. In D. Mangen & W. Peterson (Eds.), *Research instruments in social gerontology, volume two: Social roles and social participation.* Minneapolis, Minnesota: University of Minnesota Press.

Burgess, E. W. & Locke, H. J. 1955. *The family: From institution to companionship.* Second Edition. New York: American Books.

Burrus-Bammel, L. L. & Bammel, G. 1985. Leisure and recreation. In J. Birren & K. W. Schaie (Eds.), *Handbook of the psychology of aging.* New York: Van Nostrand-Reinhold.

Burton, L. & Bengtson, V. 1985. Black grandmothers: Issues of timing and continuity of roles. In V. Bengtson & J. Robertson (Eds.), *Grandparenthood.* Beverly Hills, CA: Sage.

Campbell, R. & Brody, E. 1985. Women's changing roles and help to the elderly: Attitudes of women in the U.S. and Japan. *The Gerontologist, 25,* 584-592.

Cancian, F. M. 1985. Gender politics: Love and power in the private and public spheres. In A. Rossi (Ed.), *Gender and the life course.* New York: Aldine Publishing Company.

Cancian, F. M. 1986. The Feminization of love. *Signs, 11,* 692-709.

Cantor, M. 1983. Strain among caregivers: A study of experience in the United States. *The Gerontologist, 23,* 597-604.

Cantor, M. 1979. Neighbors and friends: An overlooked resource the informal support system. *Research on Aging, 1,* 434-463.

Cath, S. 1972. Psychoanalytic viewpoints on aging: An historical survey. In D. Kent, R. Kastenbaum & S. Sherwood (Eds.), *Research planning and action for the elderly: The power and potential of social science.* New York: Behavioral Publications.

Chambre, S. M. 1984. Is volunteering a substitute for role loss in old age? An empirical test of activity theory. *The Gerontologist, 24,* 292-298.

Chappell, N. L. 1983. Informal support networks among the elderly. *Research on Aging, 5,* 77-99.

Cheal, D. J. 1988. *The gift economy.* New York: Routledge.

Cheal, D. J. 1983. Intergenerational family transfers. *Journal of Marriage and the Family, 45,* 805-814.

Cherlin, A. J. & Furstenberg, F. F. Jr. 1986. *The new American grandparent: A place in the family, a life apart.* New York: Basic Books.

Cherlin, A. J. & Furstenberg, F. F., Jr. 1985. Styles and strategies of grandparenting. In V. Bengtson & J. Robertson (Eds.), *Grandparenthood.* Beverly Hills, CA: Sage.

Chodorow, N. 1978. *The reproduction of mothering: Psychoanalysis and the sociology of gender.* Berkeley: University of California Press.

Chodorow, N. 1974. Family structure and feminine personality. In M. S. Rosaldo & L. Lamphere (Eds.), *Women, culture and society.* Palo Alto, CA: Stanford University Press.

Chown, S. M. 1981. Friendship in old age. In S. Duck & R. Gilmour (Eds.), *Personal relationships.* London: Academic Press.

Cicirelli, V. 1988. A measure of filial anxiety regarding anticipated care of elderly parents. *The Gerontologist, 28*, 478-482.

Cicirelli, V. 1984. Marital disruption and adult children's perception of their siblings' help to elderly parents. *Family Relations, 33*, 613-621.

Cicirelli, V. 1983. Adult children's attachment and helping behavior to elderly parents: A path model. *Journal of Marriage and the Family, 45*, 815-824.

Clark, R., Maddox, G. L., Shrimper, R. A. & Sumner, D. A. 1984. *Inflation and the economic well-being of the elderly.* Baltimore: John Hopkins University Press.

Clemente, F., Rexford, P. & Hirsh, C. 1972. The participation of black aged in volunteer associations. *Journal of Gerontology, 30*, 469-472.

Cohen, S. & Gans, B. 1978. *The other generation gap: The middle-aged and Their aging parents.* Chicago: Follett Publishing Company.

Committee on an Aging Society. 1986. *Productive roles in an older society.* Washington, DC: National Academy Press.

Congressional Quarterly. 1983. *Social security and retirement: Private goals and public policy.* Washington, DC: Congressional Quarterly.

Cooley, C. H. 1909. *Social organization: A study of the larger mind.* New York: Scribners.

Coser, L. 1974. *Greedy institutions: Patterns of undivided commitment.* New York: The Free Press.

Coser, L. & Coser, R. L. 1974. The housewife and her 'greedy family'. In L. Coser. *Greedy institutions: Patterns of undivided commitment.* New York: The Free Press.

Cott, N. F. 1977. *The bonds of womanhood: Woman's sphere in new england: 1780-1835.* New Haven, Connecticut: Yale University Press.

Coverman, S. 1989. Women's work is never done. In Jo Freemaned (Ed.), *Women: A feminist perspective.* Fourth edition. CA: Mayfield.

Crohan, S. E., & Antonucci, T. C. 1989. Friends as a source of social support in old age. In R.G. Adams & R. Blieszner (Eds.), *Older adult friendship*. Newbury Park: Sage.

Cross, R., Duffy, M., Warren J. & Franklin, B. 1987. Project OASIS: Volunteer mental health paraprofessionals serving nursing home residents. *The Gerontologist, 27*, 359-362.

Cumming, E. 1963. Further thoughts on the theory of disengagement. *International Social Science Journal, 15*, 377-393.

Cumming, E. & Henry, W. 1961. *Growing old: The process of disengagement.* NY: Basic Books.

Curtis, J. 1971. Volunteer association joining: A cross-national comparative note. *American Sociological Review, 36*, 872-880.

Cutler, M. E. 1977. Demographic, social-psychological and political factors in the politics of age: A foundation for research in political gerontology. *American Political Science Review, 71*, 1011-1025.

Daniels, A. K. 1987. The hidden work of constructing class and community: Women volunteer leaders in social philanthropy. In N. Gerstel & H. Gross. *Families and work*. Philadelphia: Temple University Press.

Daniels, A. K. 1985. Good times and good works: The place of sociability in the work of women volunteers. *Social Problems, 32*, 363-374.

Degler, C. 1980. *At odds: Women and the family in America from the revolution to the present.* NY: Oxford University Press.

DeVanzo, J.& Goldscheider, Frances K. 1990. Coming home again: Returns to the nest in young adulthood. *Population Studies, 44*, 241-255.

Dickens, W. & Perlman, C. 1981. Friendship over the life cycle. In S. Duck & R. Gilmour (Eds.), *Personal relations, volume two*. London: Academic Press.

DiLeonardo, M. 1987. The female world of cards and holidays: Women, families and the work of finship. *Signs, 12*, 440-453.

Dowd, J. J. 1984. Beneficence and the aged. *Journal of Gerontology, 37*, 102-108.

Dupuy, H. 1974. *Utility of the National Center for Health Statistics General Well-Being Schedule in the assessment of self representations of subjective well-being and distress.* National Conference on Education and Alcohol, Drug Abuse and Mental Health Programs. Washington, DC: U.S. Department of Health Education and Welfare.

Dye, D., Goodman, M., Roth, M., Bley, N. & Jensen, K. 1973. The older volunteer compared to the nonvolunteer. The Gerontologist, 13, 215-218.

Elinson, J. 1988. Defining and measuring health and illness. In K. W. Schaie, R. Campbell, W. Merideth, & S. Rawlings (Eds.), *Methodological issues in aging research*. NY: Springer.

Epstein, C. 1988. *Deceptive distinctions: Sex, gender and the social order.* New Haven: Yale University Press.

Erickson, E. 1977. Adulthood and world views. Paper presented at the American Academy Conference on Love and Work in Adulthood, Palo Alto.

Farrell, M.P. & Rosenberg, S. D. 1981. *Men at midlife.* Boston: Auburn House.

Ferraro, K. F. & Barresi, C. M. 1982. The impact of widowhood on the social relations of older persons. *Research on Aging, 4*, 227-249.

Ferraro, K. F., Mutran, E. & Barresi, C. M. 1984. Widowhood, health, and friendship support in later life. *Journal of Health and Social Behavior, 25*, 246-259.

Finley, N. J., Roberts, M. D. & Banahan, B. 1988. Motives and inhibitors of attitudes of filial obligations towards aging parents. *The Gerontologist, 28*, 73-78.

Fischer, C. S. 1982. *To dwell among friends: Personal networks in town and city.* Chicago: University of Chicago Press.

Fischer, C. S. & Oliker, S. J. 1983. A research note on friendship, gender and the life cycle. *Social Forces, 62*, 124-133.

Fischer, L. R. 1985. Elderly parents and the care giving role: An asymmetrical transition. In Warren A. Peterson & Jill Quadango (Eds.), *Social bonds in later life.* Beverly Hills, CA: Sage.

Fischer, L. R., Mueller, D. P. & Cooper, P. W. 1991. Older volunteers: A discussion of the Minnesota senior study. *The Gerontologist, 31*, 183-194.

Fogel, R., Hatfield, E., Kiesler, S. B. & Shanas, E. 1981. *Aging: Stability and change in the family.* NY: Academic Press.

Foskett, J. M. 1955. Social structure and social participation. *American Sociological Review, 20*, 431-438.

Fox, M., Gibbs, M. & Auerbach, D. 1985. Age and gender dimensions of friendship. *Psychology of Women Quarterly, 9*, 489-502.

Freedman, R. & Axelrod, M. 1952. Who belongs to what in a great metropolis. *Adult Leadership, 1*, 6-9.

Freud, S. 1933. Femininity. In J. Strachey (Trans. and Ed.), *New introductory lectures on psychoanalysis.* NY: Norton.

Fries, J. F. 1980. Aging, natural death, and the compression of morbidity. *New England Journal of Medicine, 303*, 130-135.

Furstenberg, F. F., Peterson, J., Nord, C. & Zill, N. 1983. The life course of children of divorce: Marital disruption and parental contact. *American Sociological Review, 48*, 656-668.

George, L. & Gwyther, L. P. 1986. Caregivers and well-being: A multidimensional examination of family caregivers of demented adults. *The Gerontologist, 26*, 253-259.

Gerstel, N. 1989. Notes towards the feminization of emotion. Paper presented at the Annual Meeting of the American Sociological Association, San Francisco, California, August.

Gerstel, N. 1988. Divorce, gender, and social integration. *Gender and Society, 2*, 343-367.

Gerstel, N. & Gallagher, S. K. 1990a. Caring for kith and kin: The effects of gender and employment. Paper presented at the Annual Meeting of the American Sociological Association, Washington, DC, August.

Gerstel, N. & Gallagher, S. K. 1990b. The third shift: Gender, caregiving and distress. Paper presented at the Annual Meeting of the Society for the Study of Social Problems, Washington, DC, August.

Gibbs, J. 1985. Family relations of the older widows and their location and importance for her social life. In Warren A. Peterson & Jill Quadango (Eds.), *Social forces in later life*. Beverly Hills, CA: Sage.

Giele, J. Z. 1980. Adulthood as transcendence of age and sex. In N. J. Smelser & E. Erickon (Eds.), *Themes of work and love in adulthood*. Cambridge, Massachusetts: Harvard University Press.

Gilligan, C. 1986. Reply. In, On *In a different voice*: An interdisciplinary forum. *Signs, 11*, 310-316.

Gilligan, C. 1982. *In a different voice: Psychological theory and women's development*. Cambridge, Massachusetts: Harvard University Press.

Girdon, B. 1978. Volunteer work and its rewards. *Volunteer Administration, 11*, 18-32.

Gitelson, M. 1948. The emotional problems of elderly people. *Geriatrics, 3*, 135-140.

Gladstone, J. W. 1988. Perceived changes in grandmother-grandchild relations following a child's separation or divorce. *The Gerontologist, 28*, 66-72.

Godbey, G. & Parker, S. 1976. *Leisure studies and services: An overview*. Philadelphia: W. B. Saunders.

Goetting, A. 1986. The developmental tasks of siblingship over the life cycle. *Journal of Marriage and the Family, 48*, 703-714.

Goode, W. 1963. *World revolution and family patterns*. NY: Free Press.

Greenberg, J. & Becker, M. 1988. Aging parents as family resources. *The Gerontologist, 28*, 786-791.

Greeno, G. & Maccoby, E. E. 1986. How different is the 'different voice'? In, On *In a different voice*: An interdisciplinary forum. *Signs, 11*, 310-316.

Gutmann, D. L. 1987. *Reclaimed powers: Towards a new psychology of men and women in later life*. NY: Basic Books.

Gutmann, D. L. 1985. The parental imperative revisited: Towards a developmental psychology of adulthood and later life. In J. A. Meacham (Ed.), *Contributions to human development*. Basel: Karger.

Gutmann, D. L. 1977. The cross cultural perspective: Notes towards a comparative psychology of aging. In J. E. Birren & K. W. Schaie (Eds.), *Handbook of the psychology of aging*. NY: Van Nostrand-Reinhold.

Hagestad, G. O. 1987a. Able elderly in the family context: changes, chances and challenges. *The Gerontologist, 27*, 417-422.

Hagestad, G. O. 1987b. Parent-child relations in later life: Trends and gaps in past research. In J. Lancaster, J. Altmann, A. Rossi, & L. Sherrod (Eds.), *Parenting across the life span: Biosocial dimensions*. NY: Adline de Gruyter.

Hagestad, G. O. 1986a. The family: Women as grandparents and kin-keepers. In A. Pifer & L. Bronte (Eds.), *Our aging society*. NY: W. W. Norton.

Hagestad, G. O. 1986b. The aging society and family life. *Daedalus, 115*, 119-140.

Hagestad, G. O. 1985. Continuity and connectedness. In V. Bengtson & J. Robertson (Eds.), *Grandparenthood*. Beverly Hills, CA: Sage.

Hagestad, G. O. 1982. Divorce: The family ripple effect. *Generations, 7*, 24-25.

Hancock, P., Mangen, D. & McChesney, K. 1988. The exchange dimension of solidarity: Measuring intergenerational exchange and functional solidarity. In D. Mangen, V. Bengtson, & P. Candry Jr. (Eds.), *Measurement of intergenerational relations*. Beverly Hills, CA: Sage.

Hausknecht, M. 1962. *The joiners: A sociological description of voluntary association membership in the United States*. NY: The Bedminster Press.

Hays, R. B. 1988. Friendship. in S. W. Duck (Ed.), *Handbook of personal relationships*. NY: John Wiley.

Heinemann, G. D. 1985. Interdependence in informal support systems: The case of elderly, urban widows. In W. A. Peterson & J. Quadango (Eds.), *Social bonds in later life: Aging and interdependence*. Beverly Hills, CA: Sage.

Held, V. 1987. Non-contractual society. *Canadian Journal of Philosophy: Science, Morality and Feminist Theory, Supplement, 13*, 111-137.

Hess, B. 1979. Sex roles, friendships and the life course. *Research on Aging, 1*, 494-515.

Hess, B. 1972. Friendship. In M. W. Riley, M. Johnson, & A. Foner (Eds.), *Aging and society: A sociology of age stratification* (Vol. 3). NY: Russell Sage Foundation.

Hetherington, E. M, Cox, M. & Cox, R. 1982. Divorced fathers. *Family Coordinator, 25*, 171-176.

Hill, R., Foote, N., Aldous, J., Carlson, R. & Donald, R. 1970. *Family development in three generations*. Cambridge, MA: Schenkman.

Hirsh, C., Kent, D. & Silverman, S. 1972. Homogeneity and heterogeneity among low-income negro and white aged. In D. Kent, R. Kastenbaum & S.Sherwood (Eds.), *Research planning and action for the elderly*. NY: Behavioral Publications.

Hochschild, A. R. 1989. *The second shift: Working parents and the revolution at home*. With Anne Machung. NY: Viking.

Hochschild, A. R. 1983. *The managed heart: Commercialization of human feeling*. Berkeley, CA: University of California Press.

Hochschild, A. R. 1979. Emotion work, feeing rules and social structure. *American Journal of Sociology, 85*, 551-575.

Hochschild, A. R. 1975. Disengagement theory: A critique and a proposal. *American Sociological Review, 40*, 553-569.

Hochschild, A. R. 1973. *The unexpected community: Portrayal of an old age subculture*. Englewood Cliffs, NJ: Prentice Hall.

Hofferth, S. 1984. Kin networks, race, and family structure. *Journal of Marriage and the Family, 46*, 791-806.

Horowitz, A. 1985a. Sons and daughters as caregivers to older parents: Differences in role performance and consequences. *The Gerontologist, 25*, 612-617.

Horowitz, A. 1985b. Family caregiving to the frail elderly. In M. P. Lawton & G. Maddox (Eds.), *Annual review of gerontology and geriatrics*. NY: Springer Publishing.

Hoyt, D., Caiser, M., Peters, G. & Babchuk, N. 1980. Life satisfaction and activity theory: A multidimensional approach. *Journal of Gerontology, 35*, 935-941.

Independent Sector. 1988. *Giving and volunteering in the United States: Summary of findings from a national survey*. Analyzed by V. Hodgkinson & M. Weitzman. Washington, DC: Independent Sector.

Institute for Social Research, 1952. *A social profile of detroit: 1952*. Ann Arbor, MI: Institute for Social Research, University of Michigan.

Jacoby, A. P. & Babchuk, N. 1963. Instrumental and expressive voluntary associations. *Sociology an Social Research, 47*, 461-471.

Jencks, C., Perman, L. & Rainwater, L. 1988. What is a good job?: A new measure of labor-market success. *American Journal of Sociology, 93*, 1322-1357.

Jenner, J. R. 1981. Volunteerism as an aspect of women's work lives. *Journal of Vocational Behavior, 19*, 302-314.

Johnson, C. L. 1988. *Ex familia: Grandparents, parents, and children adjust to divorce.* New Brunswick: Rutgers University Press.

Johnson, C. L. 1983. Fairwether friends and rainy day kin: An anthropological analysis of old age friendships in the United States. *Urban Anthropology, 12*, 103-123.

Johnson, C. L. & Catalano, D. 1981. Childless elderly and their family supports. *The Gerontologist, 21*, 610-618.

Johnson, M. 1988. *Strong mothers, weak wives: The search for gender equality.* Berkeley, CA: University of California Press.

Johnson, S. K. 1971. *Idle haven: Community building among the working-class retired.* Berkeley, CA: University of California Press.

Katz, S., Downs, T., Cash, H. & Grotz, R. 1970. Progress in the development of the index of ADL. *The Gerontologist, 10*, 20-30.

Katz, S., Ford, A. B., Moskowitz, R. W., Jackson, A. B. & Jaffe, M. W. 1963. Studies of illness in the aged: The index of ADL, a standardized measure of biological and physiological function. *Journal of the American Medical Association, 185*, 914-919.

Kelley, H. 1981. Marriage relationships and aging. In R. Fogel, E. Hatfield, S. Kiesler & E. Shanas (Eds.), *Aging: Stability and change in the family.* NY: Academic Press.

Kennedy, L. & Stokes, D. 1982. Extended family support and the high cost of housing. *Journal of Marriage and the Family, 44*, 311-318.

Kent, D., Kastenbaum, R. & Sherwood, S. 1972. *Research planning and action for the elderly: The power and potential of social science.* NY: Behavioral.

Kerber, L. K. 1986. Some cautionary words for historians. In, On *In a different voice*: An interdisciplinary forum. *Signs, 11*, 304-310.

Kivett, V. R. 1993. Racial Comparisons of the grandmother role: Implications for strengthening the family support system of older black women. *Family Relations, 42*, 165-172.

Kohen, J. 1983. Old but not alone: Informal social supports among the elderly by marital status and sex. *The Gerontologist, 23*, 57-63.

Kohlberg, L. 1966. A cognitive-developmental analysis of children's sex-role concepts and attitudes. In E. Maccoby (Ed.), *The development of sex differences.* Stanford, CA: Stanford University Press.

Komarovsky, M. 1964. *Blue-collar marriage.* NY: Random House.

Konopka, G. 1976. *Young girls: A portrayal of adolescence.* Englewood Cliffs, NJ: Prentice-Hall.

Kovar, M. G. 1977. Elderly people: The population 65 years and older. U.S. Department of Health, Education and Welfare: U.S. 1976-1977 (HEW Publication Number 77-1232). Washington, DC: Government Printing Office.

Lang, A. M. & Brody, E. M. 1983. Characteristics of middle-aged daughters and help to their elderly mothers. *Journal of Marriage and the Family, 45*, 193-202.

Lasch, C. 1977. *Haven in a heartless world: The family besieged.* NY: Basic Books.

Lawton, M. P. & Brody, E. M. 1969. Assessment of older people: Self-maintaining and instrumental activities of daily living. *The Gerontologist, 9*, 179-186.

Lee, G. 1985. Kinship and social support of the elderly: The case of the United States. *Aging and Society, 5*, 19-38.

Lee, G. & Ellithorpe, E. 1982. Intergenerational exchange and subjective well-being. *Journal of Marriage and the Family, 44*, 217-224.

Lefley, H. P. 1988. Aging parents as caregivers of mentally ill adult children: An emerging social problem. *Hospital and Community Psychiatry, 38*, 1063-1070.

Leichter, H. J. & Mitchell, W. E. 1967. *Kinship and casework.* NY: Russel Sage.

Leigh, G. 1982. Kinship interaction over the family life span. *Journal of Marriage and the Family, 43*, 197-208.

Lennon, M. C. 1987. Sex differences in distress: The impact of gender and work roles. *Journal of Health and Social Behavior, 28*, 290-305.

Leukoff, S., Cleary, P. & Wetle, T. 1987. Differences in the appraisal of health between aged and middle aged adults. *Journal of Gerontology, 42*, 114-120.

Linsk, N., Keigher, S. & Osterbusch, S. 1988. States' policies regarding paid family caregiving. *The Gerontologist, 28*, 204-212.

Litwak, E. 1985. *Helping the elderly: The complementary roles of informal networks and formal systems.* NY: The Guilford Press.

Litwak, E. & Kulis, E. 1987. Technology, proximity and measures of kin support. *Journal of Marriage and the Family, 49*, 649-661.

Liu, K., Manton, K. & Liu, B. 1985. Home care expenses for the disabled elderly. *Health Care Financing Review, 7*, 51-58.

Longino, C. & Lipman, A. 1981. Married and spouseless men and women in planned retirement communities: Support network differentials. *Journal of Marriage and the Family, 43*, 169-177.

Lopata, H. Z. 1979. *Women as widows: Support systems.* NY: Elsevier.

Lopata, H. Z. 1978. Contributions of extended families to the support systems of metropolitan area widows: Limitations of the modified kin network. *Journal of Marriage and the Family, 40*, 356-364.

Lopata, H. Z. 1973. *Widowhood in an American city.* Cambridge, MA: Schenkman Publishing Company.

Lopata, H. Z. 1970. The Social involvement of American widows. *American Behavioral Scientist, 14* 41-57.

Luria, Z. 1986. A Methodological critique. In, On *In a different voice*: An interdisciplinary forum. *Signs, 11*, 316-321.

Macken, L. L. 1986. A profile of functionally impaired elderly persons living in the community. *Health Care Financing Review, 7*, 33-49.

Maddox, G. L. 1972. Sociological perspectives in gerontological research. In D. Kent, R. Kastenbaum & S. Sherwood (Eds.), *Research planning and action for the elderly*. NY: Behavioral Publications.

Maddox, G. L. 1966. Persistence of life style among the elderly: A longitudinal study of patterns of social activity in relation to life satisfaction. *Proceedings, Seventh International Congress of Gerontology, 6*, 309-311.

Maddox, G. L. 1964. Disengagement theory: A critical evaluation. *The Gerontologist, 4*, 80-82.

Maddox, G. L. 1962. A longitudinal multidisciplinary study of human aging: Selected methodological issues. In, *Proceedings, social statistics section, American Statistical Association*.

Malson, M. R. 1983. Black families an childrearing support networks. In, *Research in the interweave of social roles: Jobs and families* (Vol. 3). Greenwich, CT: JAI Press.

Mancini, J. A. 1980. Friend interaction, competence, and morale in old age. *Research on Aging, 2*, 416-431.

Mancini, J. A. & Blieszner, R. 1989. Aging parents and adult children. *Journal of Marriage and the Family, 51*, 275-290.

Mangen, D., Bengtson, V. & Landry, P., Jr. 1988. *Measurement of intergenerational relations*. Newbury Park, CA: Sage.

Mangen, D. J. & Peterson, W. A. 1984. *Research instruments in gerontology, volume three: Health, program evaluation, and demography*. Minneapolis, MN: University of Minnesota Press.

Mangen, D. J. & Peterson, W. A. 1983. *Research instruments in gerontology, volume two: Social roles and social participation*. Minneapolis, MN: University of Minnesota Press.

Mangen, D. J. & Peterson, W. A. 1982. *Research instruments in gerontology, volume one: Clinical and social psychology*. Minneapolis, MN: University of Minnesota Press.

Matthews, S. 1986. *Friendships through the life course: Oral biographies in old age*. Beverly Hills, CA: Sage.

Matthews, S. 1983. Definitions of friendship and their consequences in old age. *Aging and society, 3*, 141-155.

Matthews, S. H. & T. T. Rosner 1988. Shared filial responsibility: The family as the primary caregiver. *Journal of Marriage and the Family, 50*, 185-195.

McCready, W. 1985. Styles of grandparenting among white ethnics. In V. Bengston & J. Robertson (Eds.), *Grandparenthood*. Beverly Hills, CA: Sage.

McGhee, J. 1985. The effects of siblings on the life satisfaction of the rural elderly. *Journal of Marriage and the Family, 47*, 47: 85-91.

McGhee, J. & Wells, K. 1982. Gender typing and androgyny in later life: New directions for theory and research. *Human Development, 25*, 116-139.

McPherson, J. M. & Smith-Lovin, L. 1986. Sex segregation in voluntary associations. *American Sociological Review, 51*, 61-79.

McPherson, J. M. & Smith-Lovin, L. 1982. Women and weak ties: Differences by sex in the size of voluntary organizations. *American Journal of Sociology, 87*, 883-903.

Miller, J. B. 1976. *Toward a new psychology of women*. Boston: Beacon Press.

Mindel, C. 1983. Kinship relations. In D. Mangen & W. Peterson (Eds.), *Research instruments in gerontology, volume two: Social roles and social participation*. Minneapolis, MN: University of Minnesota Press.

Mitchell, J. & Register, J. 1984. An exploration of family interaction with the elderly by race ses and residence. *The Gerontologist, 24*, 48-54.

Montgomery, R. J. V., Gonyea, J. G. & Hooyman, N. R. 1985. Caregiving and the experience of subjective and objective burden. *Family Relations, 34*, 19-26.

Moore, W. 1963. *Man, time and society*. NY: Wiley.

Morgan, J. 1983. The redistribution of income by family and institutions in emergency help patterns. In G. Duncan & J. Morgan (Eds.), *5000 American families*. Patterns of economic progress, Volume 10, Ann Arbor, MI: Institute for Social Research.

Morgan, L. A. 1984. Changes in family interactions following widowhood. *Journal of Marriage and the Family, 46*, 323-331.

Morgan, L. A. 1983. Intergenerational economic assistance to children: The case of widows and widowers. *Journal of Gerontology, 38*, 725-731.

Morgan, L. A. 1982. Social roles in later life: Some recent research trends, *Annual review of gerontology and geriatrics*. NY: Springer Publishing.

Morgan, L. A. 1981. Economic change at midlife widowhood: A longitudinal analysis. *Journal of Marriage and the Family, 43*, 899-907.

Morgan, L. A. 1980. Work in widowhood: A viable option. *The Gerontologist, 20*, 581-587.

Morrow-Howell, N. & Ozawa, M. N. 1987. Helping network: Services to seniors. *The Gerontologist, 27*, 17-20.

Motenko, A. K. 1989. The frustrations, gratifications, and well-being of dementia caregivers. *The Gerontologist, 27,* 166-172.

National Council on Aging. 1975. *The myth and reality of aging in America.* Washington, DC: Louis Harris and Associates.

Nelson, M. & Abel, E. K. 1990. *Circles of care: Work and identity in women's lives.* Albany: SUNY Press.

Neugarten, B. 1974. Age groups in American society and the rise of the young-old. *Annals of Political and Social Sciences, 415,* 187-189.

Noelker, L. S. 1987. Incontinence in elderly cared for by the family. *The Gerontologist, 27,* 194-200.

Norton, R. 1983. Measuring marital quality: A critical look at the dependent variable. *Journal of Marriage and the Family, 45,* 141-151.

OAVP/ACTION. 1986. *Retired senior volunteer program: Directory* (October). Washington DC: Government Printing Office.

OAVP/ACTION. 1982. ACTION's older American volunteer programs. *Prime Time.* Volume 5, Number 1. Government Printing Office. 361-804: 1002, Washington, DC: ACTION.

OAVP/ACTION. 1971. *Recommendations for developing the retired senior volunteer program.* Administration on Aging, Department of Health, Education, and Welfare, prepared by Leo K. Kramer. Washington, DC: Government Printing Office.

O'Bryant, S. L. 1988. Sibling support and older widows' well-being. *Journal of Marriage and the Family, 50,* 173-183.

O'Bryant, S. L. 1985. Neighbors support of older widows who live alone in their own homes. *The Gerontologist, 25,* 305-310.

O'Donnell, L. 1985. *The unheralded majority: Contemporary women as mothers.* Lexington, MA: Lexington.

Oliker, S. 1989. *Best friends and marriage: Exchange among women.* Berkeley, CA: University of California Press.

Ortner, S. B. & Whitehead, H. 1981. *Sexual meanings: The cultural construction of gender and sexuality.* NY: Cambridge University Press.

Ostrander, S. 1984. *Women of the upper class.* Philadelphia: Temple University Press.

Palmore, E. 1981. *Social patterns in normal aging: Findings from the Duke longitudinal study.* Durham, NC: Duke University Press.

Parsons, T. & Bales, R. F. 1955. *Family, socialization and interaction process.* Glencoe, IL: Free Press.

Payne, B. & Bull, C. 1985. The older volunteer: A case for interdependence. In W. Peterson & J. Quadango (Eds.), *Social Bonds in Later Life.* Beverly Hills, CA: Sage.

Petrowsky, M. 1976. Marital status, sex and the social networks of the elderly. *Journal of Marriage and the Family, 49,* 749-757.

Peters, G. 1983. Friends, neighbors and confidants. In D. Mangen & W. Peterson (Eds.), *Research instruments in social gerontology, volume two: Social roles and social participation.* Minneapolis, MN: University of Minnesota Press.

Pihlblad, C., & Adams, D. L. 1972. Widowhood, social participation and life satisfaction. *International Journal of Aging and Human Development, 3*, 323-330.

Pillemer, K. & Suitor, J. J. 1991. Will I ever escape my child's problems?: Effects of adult children's problems on elderly parents. *Journal of Marriage and the Family, 53*, 585-594.

Pleck, J. 1977. The work-family role system. *Social Problems, 24*, 417-427.

Powers, E. A. & Bultena, G. L. 1976. Sex differences in intimate friendships of old age. *Journal of Marriage and the Family, 38*, 739-749.

Presser, H. R. 1989. Some economic complexities of child care provided by grandmothers. *Journal of Marriage and the Family, 51*, 581-591.

Preston, S. H. 1984. Children and the elderly in the U.S.. *Scientific American, 251*, 44-49.

Prime Time. 1985. History of the foster grandparents program. Volume 8, Number 3. Washington, DC: ACTION.

Prime Time. 1984. History of the senior care program. Volume 7, Number 2. Washington, DC: ACTION.

Radloff, L. S. 1977. The CES-D scale: A self report scale for research in the general population. *Applied Psychological Measurement, 1*, 385-401.

Rawlins, W. K. 1992. *Frienship matters: Communication, dialectics, and the life course.* NY: Aldine de Gruyter.

Rawlins, W. K. 1983. Negotiating close friendships: The dialectic of conjunctive freedoms. *Human communication research, 9*, 255-266.

Reisman, J. M. 1981. Adult friendships. In S. Duck & R. Gilmour (Eds.), *Personal relationships 2: Developing personal relationships.* London: Academic Press.

Retsinas, J. & Garrity, P. 1985. Nursing home friendships. *The Gerontologist, 25*, 376-381.

Rexroat, C. & Shehan, C. 1987. The family life cycle and spouses' time in housework. *Journal of Marriage and the Family, 49*, 737-750.

Ricardo-Campbell, R. 1988. Women: Retirees and widows. In R. Ricardo-Campbell & E. Lazear (Eds.), *Issues in contemporary retirement.* Stanford, CA: Stanford University Press.

Riley, M. & Foner, A. 1968. *Aging and society: Volume one, an inventory of research findings.* NY: Russel Sage Foundation.

Rimmer, L. 1983. The economics of work and caring. In J. Finch & D. Groves (Eds.), *A labor of love.* Boston, MA: Routledge and Kegan Paul.

Roberto, K. A. & Kimboko, P. J. 1989. Friendships in later life: Definitions and maintenance patterns. *International Journal of Aging and Human Development, 28,* 9-19.

Roberto, K. A. & Scott, J. P. 1986. Friendships of older men and women: Exchange patterns and satisfaction. *Psychology and Aging, 1,* 103-109.

Roberto, K. A. & Scott, J. P. 1984. Friendship patterns among older women. *International Journal of Aging and Human Development, 19,* 1-10.

Robertson, J. F. 1977. Grandmotherhood: A study of role conceptions. *Journal of Marriage and the Family, 39,* 165-174.

Robinson, B. C. 1983. Validation of a caregiver strain index. *Journal of Gerontology, 38,* 344-348.

Rodgers, W. & Herzog, R. 1987. Interviewing older adults: The accuracy of factual information. *Journal of Gerontology, 42,* 387-394.

Rosaldo, M. Z. & Lamphere, L. 1974. *Women, culture and society.* Stanford, CA: Stanford University Press.

Rosemmayr, L. 1977. The family — A source of hope for the elderly. In E. Shanas & M. Sussman (Eds.), *Family bureaucracy and the elderly.* Durham, NC: Duke University Press.

Rosenthal, C. J. 1985. Kinkeeping in the familial division of labor. *Journal of Marriage and the Family, 47,* 965-974.

Rosow, I. 1974. *Socialization to old age.* Berkeley, CA: University of California Press.

Rosow, I. 1967. *Social integration of the aged.* NY: The Free Press.

Ross, C. & Mirowsky, J. 1988. Child care and emotional adjustment to wives' employment. *Journal of Health and Social Behavior, 29,* 127-138.

Rossi, A. 1986. Sex and gender in the aging society. In A. Piter & L. Bronte (Eds.), *Our aging society.* NY: Norton and Company.

Rossi, A. & Rossi, P. 1990. *Of human bonding.* NY: Aldine de Gruyter.

Rubin, L. 1985. *Just friends.* NY: Harper and Row.

Ruddick, S. 1984. Maternal thinking. In J. Trebilcot (Ed.), *Mothering: Essays in feminist theory.* Totowa, NJ: Rowman and Allanheld.

Schaie, K. W. 1988. Methodological issues in aging research: An introduction. In K. W. Schaie, S. Campbell, W. Meridith, & S. Rawlings (Eds.), *Methodological issues in aging research.* NY: Springer.

Schaie, K. W. & Herzog, L. 1985. Measurement in the psychology of adulthood and aging. In J. Birren & K. Schaie (Eds.), *Handbook on the psychology of aging.* Second Edition. NY: Van Nostrand-Reinhold.

Scharlach, A. 1988. Peer counselor training for nursing home residents. *The Gerontologist, 28,* 499-502.

Scharlach, A. 1987. Role strain in mother-daughter relationships in later life. *The Gerontologist, 27,* 627-631.

Scharlach, A. E. & Boyd, S. L. 1989. Caregiving and employment: Results of an employer survey. *The Gerontologist, 29*, 382-387.

Schorr, A. L. 1960. *Filial responsibility of the american family.* Washington, DC: Social Security Administration, Department of Health, Education and Welfare.

Schulman, N. 1975. Life-cycle variation in patterns of close relationships. *Journal of Marriage and the Family, 37*, 813-821.

Schulz, R. 1990. Theoretical perspectives on caregiving: Concepts, variables, and methods. In D.E. Biegel & A. Blum (Eds.), *Aging and caregiving: Theory, research and policy.* Newbury Park, CA: Sage.

Schulz, R., Visintainer, P. & Williamson, G. M. 1990. Psychiatric and physical morbidity effects of caregiving. *Journal of Gerontology, 45*, P181-191.

Scott, J. C., Jr. 1957. Membership and participation in voluntary associations. *American Sociological Review, 22*, 315-326.

Scott, J. P. 1983. Siblings and other kin. In T. H. Brubaker (Ed.), *Family Relationships in later life.* Beverly Hills, CA: Sage.

Shanas, E. 1980. Older people and their families: The new pioneers. *Journal of Marriage and the Family, 42*, 9-15.

Shanas, E. 1979a. Social myth as hypothesis: The case of the family relations of old people. *The Gerontologist, 19*, 3-9.

Shanas, E. 1979b. The family as a social support system in old age. *The Gerontologist, 19*, 3-9.

Shanas, E. 1977. *National survey of the aged: 1975.* Chicago, IL: University of Illinois, Chicago Circle.

Shanas, E. 1973. Family-kin networks and aging in cross-cultural perspective. *Journal of Marriage and the Family, 35*, 505-511.

Shanas, E., Streib, G. F. 1965. *Social structure and the family: Generational relations.* Englewood Cliffs, NJ: Prentice-Hall.

Shanas, E. & Sussman, M. 1981. The family in later life: Social structure and social policy. In R. Fogel, E. Hatfield, S. Kiesler, & E. Shanas (Eds.), *Aging: Stability and change in the family.* NY: Academic Press.

Shanas, E., and Townsend, P. (968). *Older people in three industrial societies.* NY: Atherton Press.

Sharpley, C. & Cross, D. 1982. A psychometric dvaluation of the Spainer dyadic adjustment scale. *Journal of Marriage and the Family, 44*, 739-741.

Shea, L, Thompson, L. & Blieszner, R. 1988. Resources in older adults' old and new friendships. *Journal of Social and Personal Relationships, 5*, 83-96.

Sherwin, S. 1989. Ethics, feminism and caring. *Queens Quarterly, 96*, 3-13.

Shorter, E. 1975. *The making of the modern family.* NY: Basic Books.

Silverman, P. R. 1986. *Widow-to-widow.* NY: Springer Publishing Company.

Simpson, I. H. & McKinney, J. 1966. *Social aspects of aging.* Durham, NC: Duke University Press.

Simpson, J. & Willwerth, J. 1989. For goodness' sake, *Time.* January 9, pp. 20-24.

Sinnot, J. D. 1984. Older men, older women: Are their perceived sex roles similar? *Sex Roles, 10,* 847-856.

Sinnot, J. D. 1982. Correlates of sex roles of older adults. *Journal of Gerontology, 37,* 587-594.

Sinnot, J. D. 1977. Sex-role constancy, biology and successful aging. *The Gerontologist, 17,* 459-463.

Smith, D. H. 1975. Voluntary action and voluntary groups. *Annual review of sociology.* Volume One. Palo Alto, CA: Annual Reviews Inc.

Smith, J. 1966. The narrowing social world of the aged. In Ida H. Simpson & John C. McKinney (Eds.), *Social aspects of aging.* Durham, NC: Duke University Press.

Smith-Rosenberg, C. 1975. The female world of love and ritual: Relations between women in 19th century america. *Signs, 1* 1-29.

Soldo, B. J., & Sharma, M. 1980. Families who purchase vs families who provide care services to Elderly Relatives. Paper Presented at the 33rd Annual Meeting of the Gerontological Society of America, San Diego, California.

Spitze, G. & Logan, J. 1992. Helping as a component of parent-adult child relations. *Research on Aging, 14,* 291-312.

Spitze, G. & Logan, J. 1989. Gender differences in family support: Is there a payoff? *The Gerontologist, 29,* 109-113.

Stack, C. B. 1986. The culture of gender: Women and men of color. In, On *In a different voice*: An interdisciplinary forum. *Signs, 11,* 321-24.

Stack, C. B. 1974. *All our kin: Strategies for survival in the black community.* NY: Harper and Row.

Stahl, S. M. 1984. Health. In D. Mangen & W. Peterson (Eds.), *Research instruments in social gerontology, volume three: Health, program evaluation, and demography.* Minneapolis, MN: University of Minnesota Press.

Steinfels, M. 1980. Women volunteers from 1860 to the present: An historical sketch and modest critique. In United Hospital Fund, *Women, volunteering and health policy.* NY: United Hospital Fund of New York.

Stoller, E. P. 1985. Exchange patterns in the informal support networks of the elderly: The impact of reciprocity on morale. *Journal of Marriage and the Family, 47,* 335-342.

Stoller, E. P. 1983. Parental caregiving by adult children. *Journal of Marriage and the Family, 45,* 851-858.

Stoller, E. P. & Earl, L. L.   1983.   Help with activities of everyday life: Sources of support for the non-institutionalized elderly.   *The Gerontologist, 23*, 64-70.

Stoller, E. P. & Pugliesi, K.   1989.   Other roles of caregivers: Competing responsibilities and supportive resources. *Journals of Gerontology, 44*, S231-238.

Stone, R., Cafferata, G. L. & Sangl, J.   1987.   Caregivers of the frail elderly: A national profile. *The Gerontologist, 27*, 616-626.

Streib, G.   1965.   Intergenerational relations: Perspectives of the two generations on the older parent. *Journal of Marriage and the Family, 27*, 469-476.

Streib, G. & Beck, R. W. 1980. Older families: A decade review. *Journal of Marriage and the Family, 42*, 937-958.

Sudman, S. 1983. Applied sampling. In P. Rossi, J. Wright, & A. Anderson (Eds.), *Handbook of survey research.* NY: Academic Press.

Szinovacz, M. 1989. Retirement, couples, and household work. In S. Bahr & E. Peterson (Eds.), *Aging and the family.* Lexington, MA: Lexington Books.

Thompson, E. H. & Doll, W. 1982. The burden of families coping with the mentally ill: An invisible crisis. *Family Relations, 31*, 379-388.

Thompson, L. & Walker, A. 1989. Gender in families: Women and men in marriage, work, and parenthood. *Journal of Marriage and the Family, 51*, 845-871.

Tinsley, B. R. & Parke, R. D. 1984. Grandparents as support and socialization agents. In M. Lewis (Ed.), *Beyond the dyad.* NY: Plenum.

de Tocqueville, A. 1956. *Democracy in America.* NY: Mentor.

Townsend, P. 1957. *The family life of old people: An inquiry in east London.* Foreword by J. H. Sheldon. Glencoe: Free Press.

Troll, L. E. 1986. *Family issues in current gerontology.* Current Gerontology Series Robert C. Atchley (Ed.), NY: Springer Publishing Company.

Troll, L. E. 1983. Grandparents: The family watchdogs. In T. Brubaker (Ed.), *Family relations in later life.* Beverly Hills, CA: Sage.

Troll, L. E. 1971. The family of later life: A decade review. *Journal of Marriage and the Family, 37*, 263-290.

Troll, L. E., Miller, S. J. & Atchley, R. C. 1979. *Families in later life.* Belmont, CA: Wadsworth.

Troll, L. E. & Smith, J. 1976. Attachment through the life-span: Some questions about dyadic bonds among adults. *Human Development, 19*, 156-170.

Troll, L. E. & Stapley, J. 1986. Elders and the extended family system: Health, family salience and affect. In J. Munnich (Ed.), *Life span and change in gerontological perspective.* NY: Academic Press.

Tronto, J. C. 1987. Beyond gender difference to a theory of care. *Signs, 12,* 644-663.

Turner, B. F. 1982. Sex-related differences in aging. In B. B. Wolman (Ed.), *Handbook of developmental psychology.* Englewood Cliffs, NJ: Prentice-Hall.

U. S. Bureau of the Census. 1990. *Statistical abstract of the United States: 1990.* 110th Edition. Washington, DC: Government Printing Office.

U. S. Bureau of the Census. 1988. *Who's helping out?: Support networks among American families.* Current Population Reports, Series P-70, Number 13, Washington, DC: Government Printing Office, October.

U. S. Bureau of the Census. 1971. *1970 census of population, classified index of industries and occupations.* Washington, DC: Government Printing Office.

U. S. Bureau of Labor Statistics. 1989. Bulletin 2096. In *Statistical abstract of the United States: 1988.* Table 623. Washington, DC: Government Printing Office.

U.S. Congress, Senate. 1989. Senator Nunn, Speaking for the Citizenship and National Service Act of 1989. Proceedings and Debates of the 101st Congress, first session, January 25. *Congressional Record.* No. 6, Part III.

U. S. Congress, Senate. 1969. An act to amend the Older Americans Act of 1965, and for other purposes. P.C. 91-69, Ninty-First Congress, H.R. 11235, September 17, 1969. Washington, DC: Government Printing Office.

U. S. Department of Health and Human Services. 1986. Aging America: Trends and projections, 1985-1986. U.S. Senate Special Committee on Aging in Conjunction with the American Association of Retired Persons, the Federal Council on Aging and the Administration of Aging. Washington, DC: Government Printing Office.

U.S. Department of Labor. 1988. Employment in perspective: Women in the labor force. Report 88-4391, Bureau of Labor Statistics. Washington, DC: Government Printing Office.

U.S. President, Bush, George. 1989. *Inaugural address.* Transcript printed in the New York Times, Saturday, January 21, 1989, p. 10.

U.S. Social Security Administration. 1987. *Social security bulletin.* (June). In *Statistical abstract of the United States: 1988.* Table 554. Washington, DC: Government Printing Office.

Uhlenberg, P. 1988. Population aging and the timing of old-age benefits. In R. Ricardo-Campbell & E. P. Lazear (Eds.), *Issues in contemporary retirement.* Stanford, CA: Hoover Institute.

Verbrugge, L. M. 1983. A research note on adult friendship contact: A dyadic perspective. *Social Forces, 62,* 78-83.

Viscusi, W. K. 1981. An assessment of aid to the elderly: Incentive effects and the elderly's role in society. In R. Fogel, E. Hatfield, S. Kiesler, & E. Shanas (Eds.), *Aging: Stability and change in the family.* NY: Academic Press.

Waite, L. J. & Harrison, S. C. 1992. Keeping in touch: How women in mid-life allocate social contacts among kith and kin. *Social Forces, 70,* 637-655.

Walker, A. & Thompson, L. 1983. Intimacy and intergenerational aid and contact among mothers and daughters. *Journal of Marriage and the Family, 54,* 841-849.

Wan, T. & Odell, G. 1983. Major role loss and social participation of older males. *Research on Aging, 5,* 173-196.

Weber, M. 1947. *From Max Weber: Essays in sociology.* Edited and Translated by H. H. Gerth & E. Wright Mills. NY: Oxford University Press.

Weeks, J. R. & Cuellae, J. 1981. The role of family members in the helping networks of older people. *The Gerontologist, 21,* 388-395.

Weg, R. B. 1983. *Sexuality in later years: Rules and behavior.* NY: Academic Press.

Welter, B. 1966. The cult of true womanhood: 1820-1860. *American Quarterly, 18,* 151-174.

Wilensky, H. 1964. Life cycle, work situations and participation in formal associations. In R. W. Kleemeier (Ed.), *Aging and leisure.* NY: Oxford University Press.

Wilensky, H. 1961. Orderly careers and social participation. *American Sociological Review, 26,* 521-539.

Wiseman, J. P. 1986. Friendship: Bonds and binds in a voluntary relationship. *Journal of Social and Personal Relationships, 3,* 191-211.

Wood, V. & Robertson, J. 1978. Friendship and kinship interaction: Differential effect of morale of the elderly. *Journal of Marriage and the Family, 44,* 367-375.

Wright, P. 1989. Gender differences in adult's same-and cross-gender friendships. In R. G. Adams & R. Blieszner (Eds.), *Older adult friendship.* Newbury Park: Sage.

Youmans, E. G. 1967. Family disengagement among older urban and rural women. *Journal of Gerontology, 22,* 209-211.

Young, R. F. & Kahana, E. 1989. Specifying caregiving outcomes: Gender and relationship aspects of caregiver strain. *The Gerontologist, 29,* 660-666.

Index

About the Author

SALLY K. GALLAGHER is an Assistant Professor of Sociology at Oregon State University. Her dissertation research on care giving received the 1993 Dissertation Award from the American Sociological Association Section on Aging.